Under a Silky Sky:

The Symbolist Poetry of Edith Covensky

A selection of other books by Yair Mazor:

Hounding the Hound of the Baskervilles
A Poetic Portrait of the Detective Novel

Poetic Acrobat:
The Poetry of Ronny Someck

Nocturnal Lament:
The Poetry of David Fogel and Modern Hebrew Poetry

Broken Twig:
The Poetry of Dalia Ravikovich and Modern Hebrew Poetry

Bridled Bird:
The Poetry of Nathan Zach and Modern Hebrew Poetry

The Flower and the Fury:
The Poetry of Yonah Wollach and Modern Hebrew Poetry

Who Wrought the Bible? Unveiling the Bible's Aesthetic Secrets

Israeli Poetry of the Holocaust

Somber Lust: The Art of Amos Oz"

Pain, Pining, and Pine Trees: Contemporary Hebrew Poetry

The Triple Cord: Agnon, Hamsun, Strindberg:
Where Hebrew and Scandinavian Meet

The Poetry of Asher Reich: Portrait of a Hebrew Poet

Forthcoming books:

The Cryptic Bible: The Bible Surrenders Its Aesthetic Secrets

A Poem Writes Poetry: The Hebrew Poetry of Ronny Sommeck

Under a Silky Sky:

The Symbolist Poetry of Edith Covensky

Yair Mazor

Milwaukee, Wisconsin

Illustrations and painting used with permission from the artists and as credited.

Poems translated from the Hebrew by Edouard Codish
Manuscript text translated by Marganit Rotman-Weinberger
Cover art by Arie Menes, www.ariemenes.com

Published by
MavenMark Books
an imprint of HenschelHAUS Publishing, Inc.
www.henschelHAUSbooks.com

ISBN: 978159598-307-7
E-ISBN: 978159598-308-4
LCCN: 2014954341

Publisher's Cataloging-In-Publication Data
(Prepared by The Donohue Group, Inc.)

Mazor, Yair, 1950-
Under a silky sky : the Symbolist poetry of Edith Covensky / Yair Mazor ; poems translated from the Hebrew by Edouard Codish ; manuscript text translated by Marganit Rotman-Weinberger.

pages : illustrations ; cm

Includes information on access to additional downloadable content at publisher's website.
Includes bibliographical references.
Issued also as an ebook.
ISBN: 978-1-59598-307-7

1. Ḳovensḳi, Idit, 1945---Criticism and interpretation. 2. Ḳovensḳi, Idit, 1945---Translations into English. 3. Hebrew poetry--History and criticism. 4. Hebrew poetry--Translations into English. I. Codish, Edouard, translator.

PJ5054.K597 Z75 2015
892.46   2014954341

Printed in the United States of America.

This book is also for Bilha

TABLE OF CONTENTS

I never have any rules to follow.
I follow myself.
(Milton Avery)

POETIC PORTRAIT:
INTRODUCTION TO THE
SYMBOLIST POETRY
OF EDITH COVENSKY

I embody the poem
Feel it not just in my head
But in my mouth, too
Words have such power.
(Edith Covensky)

Reading the diverse Hebrew poems of Edith Covensky is like embarking on a speedy and turbulent train ride: one is bound to be overwhelmed by the gorgeous landscape, spellbinding sights, and ever-changing scenery. Colorful metaphors seem to chase one another in quick succession; images and expressions of feelings are generated at breakneck pace, revealing sources from which the poetry of Edith Covensky draws its aesthetic qualities.

These sources of influence are Italian Futurism, French Symbolism, and Anglo-American Stream of Consciousness (in prose fiction). And yet these literary influences detected in Edith Covensky's poetry in no way detract from or diminish her originality. Perhaps it is more accurate to talk about affinities between those three literary schools and Edith Covensky's poetry.

However, even if Edith Covensky were not influenced by these three literary schools, even if she had never heard of these three literary schools (which is highly unlikely), her affinities with them (quite limited in the case of Futurism) are evident and unmistakable.

Rich feelings, compelling emotions, appealing images, an intricate net of associations, the literary and artistic wealth of the poetic text, detailed *ars poetica*, describing the way in which the poem is conceived, powerful metaphors moving swiftly from one image to another—all these, and much more, make up the dense texture of Edith Covensky's lyrical writing. They are the main characteristics of her poetry, though certainly not the only ones, as will be demonstrated in this introductory chapter and the subsequent one.

Attempting to trace causal or "logical" or even temporal connections among the colorful images, metaphors, and metonyms that populate Covensky's poems may prove a frustrating experience. The poems use language to convey feelings, to portray emotions and experience, which cannot be described or conveyed by a "lay language."

Edith Covensky's poetry bypasses this obstacle by using vigorous flowing images that evoke feelings, emotions, associations, metaphors, metonyms, literary, and artistic allusions. I address this aspect of her poetry when discussing Edith Covensky's Symbolist (as well as other) affiliations. This is particularly relevant in view of the apparent lack of connections among the disparate components of her poems.

The common denominator among the various components of a particular poem, the one element that confers integration and unity on the text is not easily detectable.

And yet Covensky's poems are not devoid of cogent inner unity, which can be detected and revealed through a process of careful analysis and insightful interpretation. In this respect, Edith Covensky's poetry brings to mind a delicately woven embroidery or intricate lace, with its own internal pattern or "mechanism" of operation. The poems call for a thorough and meticulous study, which eventually yields the most rewarding insights. It is a worthy exercise and a gratifying experience.

Analysis of recurring motifs in Edith Covensky's poetry will yield the following components: extensive images, sensual expressions, colorful metaphors and statements, compelling, unexpected images, the color yellow, the color blue, sun, love, night, darkness, rapid transitions between poetic elements, a first-person lyrical narrator who is pining to free herself from earthly chains, who is yearning to elevate herself from the frustrating limitation of worldly bondage, the theme of creation (both cosmic and verbal, while the verbal creation aspires to echo the celestial, cosmic, divine creation); the earthly, lyrical narrator wishes to be compared to the celestial creator, a wish that is doomed to failure.

There are also elements of amusement and joy: flowers, stars, fear, light, pain, pining, sea, illusions,

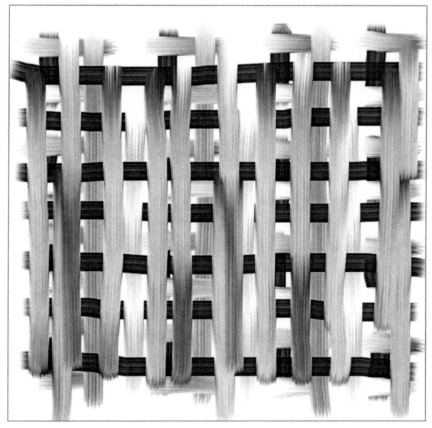

Arie Menes, Composition #05011306 ©

sinking, flowing, mother, sea, *ars poetica* (the creative process of composing a poem), a sense of fluidity, passion, sweeping vitality, associations, birds, wandering, sinking, dreams, awareness of the pain involved in composing poetry, dreams, wandering, stars, loneliness, night, summer, God, engulfing, enfolding, wind, music, time, drawing, language, word, longing, yearning, circling, revolving, water, laughter, memory, eruption, darkness, night, amusement, clamor.

These elements operate simultaneously on two levels: they endow the poem with a vivid, vital, captivating quality, sensual colors and sweeping images, while at the same time, helping to integrate and cement together the textual components of the poem, components that at first glance seem to be hopelessly disparate and devoid of common denominator or unity. Thus, the poem communicates with the reader on two parallel levels, conferring on the reading process a pleasing and gratifying intricacy.

In view of the above, it is quite evident that the poetry of Edith Covensky reflects influences and inspiration by the following literary schools: Futurist poetry, Symbolist poetry, and Stream of Consciousness in prose fiction (both in lyrical and psychological novels). These three movements make extensive use of metaphorical, metonymic, and associative principles of unity to bring together the various literary components, while at the same time suppressing the more logical, rational, temporal, and causal elements of unity.

However, this in no way suggests that the poetry of Edith Covensky is entirely Futuristic, or Symbolic, or that it follows slavishly the *ars poetica* of Stream of Consciousness. It would be more accurate to say that it embraces selective aesthetic aspects associated with the three schools of poetry and prose fiction (her affinity for Futurist poetry is the most limited one, while her affinity for Symbolist poetry is the most prevalent and complex one). Thus, her poetry cleverly adopts the only aesthetic aspects (of other schools of art of literature) that are in congruence with her own art of poetry and aesthetic practice. To be sure, such "borrowing" neither detracts from nor obscures the striking originality of the poetry of Edith Covensky.

A point of clarification: "legitimate" influential material can be an impetus to new originality. An artist exposes himself/herself to influential works of art, not because those works contain something alien to her/his own work. An artist typically borrows from material that has affinity to his/her own works of art. Thus, the influenced poet/author/artist uses the influential material as a springboard from which to launch his/her own process of original creativity. The influential materials enable the influenced artist to create and mold his/her own art while infusing it with originality. It is a source of inspiration that engenders new originality.

What follows is a brief discussion of the aesthetic characteristics of the three aforementioned literary schools that serve as inspiration to much of the poetry of Edith Covensky.

As I shall later demonstrate, although the three literary schools under consideration are distinct from each other, they have at least one notable common denominator, and together they can be seen as the source of inspiration and influence for much of Covensky's prolific literary output.

These three influential schools of poetics are: Italian Futurism, French Symbolism, and Anglo-American Stream of Consciousness (in prose fiction). Their presence in Covensky's work is undeniable: her own *ars poetica* reflects her affinity for these historic

artistic movements. Futurism, however, (mostly Italian and Russian) is the least influential of the three.

Futurism was introduced to the public when the Italian artist Tommaso Marinetti published (in 1909) the first manifesto proclaiming new trends in art, as well as a new social credo. According to Marinetti and his followers, poetry must be a hammering fist, in contrast to Symbolist poetry, which advocated subdued serenity and may be metaphorically portrayed as a soft caress at dusk.

Futurism preached admiration for the speedy, noisy machines in modern factories. Futurism celebrated aggressiveness, violence, untamed desires. It called for the abolition and delegitimization of previous schools of art. Futurism lauded war, force, and brutality, and despised earlier traditions, such as French Symbolism, which it deemed soft and effete. By contrast, Futurism placed the highest praise on dynamics and force, celebrating the black smoke gushing out of factory chimneys, rough masculinity, patriotism, devastating tempests, both natural and societal. It rejected gentle, subtle, tender poetry (as well as other forms of art and style) and welcomed thunder and might and the most challenging and extreme human activities (in both life and art), as well as assertion, aggression, and intense and radical experiences.

Futurism advocated war and spurned peace. Futurist art desired to fashion a new, modern tradition of art, to destroy and replace all previous traditions and ways of life. Consequently, Futurist poetry felt compelled to challenge the traditional, rational and causal connections that governed the components of traditional poetry and replace them with violent elements devoid of causality, progression, gradual evolution or harmony. Random, arbitrary links, and lack of integration marked the new art form.

On the whole, Covensky's poetry pays homage to Symbolist poetry, yet in one respect it adopts some of the tenets of Futurism. This has to do with the use of phrases, images, colors, and themes in the creation of atmosphere and impression. Her poems eschew the traditional structure with its causality, evolution, and temporal progression. Thus, in both Futurist poems and in Edith Covensky's poems, the text conveys the impression that its poetic components are an amalgam of random and arbitrary elements, devoid of integrating, harmonizing connections that unite the poem's fabric.

Thus, although Covensky's poetry is by no means Futuristic poetry, it is worth noting that she enlists one Futurist practice: to wit, she dispenses with logical, causal, integrative links that may connect the components of the literary text. However, that seeming lack on the surface layer of the poems is compensated by internal, underlying connections that integrate the poem's diverse components. These covert internal connections can be unearthed and unveiled through an attentive and careful process of interpretation.

As I shall demonstrate later, the lack of obvious causality and progression in Covensky's poems invites a process that unearths another kind of integrative textual unity that combines the components of the poem into a unified whole. The way in which

Edith Covensky's poetry adopts others' literary strategies will be discussed in detail later. Suffice it to say here that Covensky elects to borrow certain aesthetic techniques from other schools of poetry and prose in order to meet the requirements of her own poetry while rejecting other aspects that do not correspond to her aesthetics.

It is the task of the literary investigator to explain why certain aspects of a specific literary school have been adopted by an artist, while others have been rejected. However, the very act of adoption or of being influenced by certain trends in turn leads to a burst of original creation. The influence becomes a source of innovation and creativity.

The following quotations from a noted Futurist poem exhibits the lack of "logical," causal, temporal, developmental or harmonious principle that typifies Futurist poems (this applies also to Edith Covensky's poems).

The verses are taken from a very long poem, "Cloud in Trousers," by the Russian Futurist poet Vladimir Mayakovsky.

> "*...On the ground floor the plaster fell down.*
> *Nerves –*
> *Big,*
> *Small,*
> *Tens thousands! –*
> *Jumping dumbstruck,*

And they already called to attention:
The nerves have collapsing legs!

People smell
The scent of broiled meat in their nostrils!
Temptations such as these,
Beaming!
In helmets!
Tell the firefighters:
You cannot enter with boots on!
They climb on a burning heart
While being caressed.

Leave me alone.
I will roll barrels –
I will roll my eyes filled with tears ...”

The following examples are by the Russian poet Anna Akhmatova. Akhmatova is known as an Acmeist poet, affiliated with the Russian poetry school that opposed "misty" Symbolist poetry and advocated precision and minimalism of language, as well as the depiction of daily routine and reality. However, Akhmatova also wrote poetry that contains elements of Futurist poetry, i.e., the deliberate lack of causal, "logical"—as well as temporal and developmental—connections among the various components of the poem.

In Futurist poetry, this aspect is manifest in the use of unexpected, swift, drastic shifts from one theme to the other, from one image to the next, from one metaphor to another. The more bristly, aggressive

Arie Menes, Composition #02261407 ©

credo of Futurist poetry, however, had not been adopted by Akhmatova; she borrowed from the Russian Futurists only the deliberate avoidance of causal, logical progression between components of the poem.

IN THE EVENING

The sounds of music in the garden
Carried agony that cannot be uttered,
And the crisp, sharp breeze of the sea –
Shells on the ice which arrived on ice

"I am a faithful friend" – he stressed,
He touched my dress in that shade.
What did not were his caresses
Was the touch of those hands

This way one caresses a bird, a cat ,
Watching this way straight up her-riders....
Only through light golden eyelids in
Laughter in serene eyes

And sound of violin through sound of laments
A veil of ascending smoke:
Praise heavens: only you alone
For the first time with your loved one.

The following poems (originally written in Hebrew) seem to display in a nutshell the Futurist tendencies adopted by Edith Covensky's poetry: the lack of causal and/or "logical" and/or temporal and/or developmental connections among the different statements and images along the textual continuum of the poem. To be sure, that lack of causal, temporal, "logical" connections among the poem's various components is compensated, in Edith Covensky's poetry, by the use of different kinds of covert "cryptic" connections, such as metaphorical connections, associations, and metonyms that serve as uniting and integrating principles.

Note that an entire poem may consist of one extended image, a feeling, or a cluster of associations. Edith Covensky's poetry seems to deliberately omit any causal connections (which might confer on the text a sense of temporal evolution, of gradual development), replacing those causal, temporal connections with concealed "spatial" connections in order to express her own poetic credo. The covert cryptic unifying principle can be exposed and appreciated through the systematic process of close reading and interpretation.

The following poems demonstrate the way in which Edith Covensky's poetry replaces surface unity consisting of causality, temporality and conventional logic with another kind of unity, an internal unity based on "spatial" connections of affinity, such as associations, metonyms, metaphors, analogies, and other integrative links, including the lyrical narrator's state of mind and mood.

A CONFUSED DAY

My day twists with desire
Between hot words of summer
Revolving in a time of great yearning.

I return to the poem
Playing childish games
Drawing a bird
And a flower turning into sound.

You amuse me with the tension of a
*   confused day*
Floating from silence to silence
Remembered like a thought of the night.

WORDS IN BLUE

I pretend rhymes in refined pain
And desire captive in my memory
Bursts my supposing joyfully
Teasing my lips.

My love joins the suggestions of the poem
Heaven descends to earth
Drenched in sun
Portrayed from the apex of the day.

And then I slip pit of fear
Dense in light and noise and mountain
Portraying words in blue
Flowing in a poem like this.

The next poem is of particular interest because it contains some of the leading motifs in the poetry of Edith Covensky. Among them are the color blue, the color yellow/the sun, love, transitions in the mind of the lyrical narrator, passion, light, the creative process of composing poetry, the *ars poetica* that governs and drives her poetry, pain, fear, descending, sky, joyfulness, the flowing of feelings (as well as of images and metaphors).

A DRUNKEN BIRD

My mother collects my thoughts
Strokes a flower between scents and shadows
Pouring yellow light.

And I still play in the sun
Huddling to her bosom among souvenirs
A violin within violin .

How I catch her singing
Summarizing my childhood in complex words
Upset in this chronology
Whistling in the wind like a drunken bird.

I RUN BAREFOOT ON THE SAND

I run barefoot on the sand
Rolling like the sun in its course
In a summer wind
Close to water
Scattering hints
Like a princess by the sea.

In fact, I am a post-modern poet
Playing in the light with porcelain and flowers
Silent in the great noise
As a gesture to the poem.

A FLYING GAZELLE

You carefully inhabit my pages
Between Fantasies
Fly like a gazelle
In the summation of flowing day
Rising in memory.

I experience love
Laid on the page
Hardening in an illusory drawing
Tempting with magic
A remnant among the words.

The stars unsettle among my yearnings
Falling at the end of dreams.

POLYPHONICS

Your voice is heard clearly
Among dusky groans speaking to me in the night
Passing over the routine of my time.

I write in visionary light
My language an open sore
Among atoms of a vague moments.

My illusion floats in brush strokes
Celebrating a new abstraction at daybreak
Compressed in pain and joy
Sketching a flower.

And I exult in the midst of temptation with
quivering lip
Attached to this narration
Trapped in the poem
Among components of Polyphonic biography
Singing to myself.

MY DAY ESCAPES INTO
THE MIDST OF THE NIGHT

I continue to write the poem
In naked darkness
And shortness of time
Musing with heavy eyes
On the beauty of the moment.

Wrinkles of my forehead drop
*   on an ancient page*
Among troops of light
Fortified in routine
Crowded in these lines
As if in the mind.

My day falls on my eyelids
Wandering in dim light
Escapes into the midst of night
As if bursting out in crystalline silence
Illusory in this book.

PSYCHOSIS

My thought is wild
Erupting from the quiet
In a city of gardens
And in verses opening the poem.

I erase time
In the sinking of night begetting stars
As if returning the light to me.

My dream curls in longing
Passes with a low hurry like grass
In a psychosis floating in a new sadness.

Here the earth is closer to heaven like a bird.

ALBATROSS

My poem wanders
In the region of a time like this
Rambles in illusion
Swept off at the end of a yellow day.

And my love yearns for exile
In glowing loneliness
Drawn from my dream.

How I sort out stars
Flying at the end of time
Like a beaten bird
An albatross gliding out to sea.

And then I sink into water
Like an archeologist stepping under
            the earth's crust
Plowed with words flowing in the poem.

I SEE A DIFFERENT SUN

My love grows cleaner from volume to volume
Accumulating in subjective silence
Playing amidst the yearnings
And amusements
With such precision.

My eyes submerge in darkness
Indifferent to the night
Between gleaming stars
Childish.

I see a different sun
A new creation
Bound in a large measure of pain
Devoted to me in a myth
Stone upon stone.

And I need the words
That combine to a picture of music
Scattered thriving in a careful time
Stealthy in this clarity.

MY DAY IS MARKED IN THE RAIN

My day is marked in the rain
Between Musings rolling towards
      absurd thought
Impressive in a fluent language
Of tension and renewal.

I flow in a sea of syntheses
Like Sisyphus challenged carelessly
      in darkness.

How I seize time
Confused in the hour of writing
Chattering in a still drawing
Circling in heaven.

The stars are only a symbol of the
      center of the night
Ascending amidst the shadows
Breaking up in this cycle
Combining within me.

FOR EZRA POUND

I lean over the page
Fragile amidst thrifty syllables
Arising in tumult
Joining in the middle of the night
In a new pain absorbed with me.

I am made of words
Like chatter echoing in the dark
Brilliant in distant eternity.

My eyes are open
Turn in the spark that remains
Cling to the wind
Absurd against the day.

ODE

My love is borne up in memory
Established in this withdrawal
Bedecked in the gaiety of summer
Addicted pure to the sun.

And my excitement is marvelous
In a converging story
Caught like chance harmony in a tune
Uniting in such a drawing of desire.

And then I walk to the edge of the night
Elegantly mingle with the poem
Touching things in the symmetry of day
Broken in the sea.

CLAUSTROPHOBIA

The night becomes for me a possible reality
Minimal in silence
Among slippery bellflowers
As if invited to a dance.

And I break in the fractures
Manage to speak words
Strain to deceive myself
Erasing my shadow in an open notebook
Among imaginary flowers
In an almost claustrophobic room.

YELLOW SAND

I steal the sun for myself
Flowing with the force of light
Curl among the colors
A confounded philosopher in the summer.

My poem is printed with modern frenzy
Like an open postcard
Rolling on the margins
Holding final words.

And then I shriek during that time
Strolling among stars
Drawing more symbols with wondrous ceremony
Like words on yellow sand.

As previously suggested, the poetry of Edith Covensky corresponds to two schools of poetry and one of prose-fiction. In the case of Symbolist poetry, however, its influence on Edith Covensky's *ars poetica* is much more extensive than the influence of Futurist poetry, for it is associated with different layers of the poetic text. Similarly, the influence of the Stream of Consciousness movement displayed by Edith Covensky's poetry is much more intricate than her relation to Futurist poetry. In fact, her affinity for Symbolist poetry is the most pronounced.

Symbolism as a literary movement (as well as in other media, notably painting) was introduced during the last two decades of the 19th century. In 1886, the French poet Jean Moreas published the first manifesto of literary Symbolism, in the French newspaper *Le Figaro*. As in the case of almost every new artistic school, Symbolism rebelled against the poetic credo and practice of both Realism and Naturalism.

Whereas Realism and Naturalism aimed at depicting concrete, everyday reality in as minute and accurate detail as possible, Symbolism desired to map poetically the hidden, imaginary, mysterious layers of reality, the ones that cannot be conveyed by obvious logical means. That hidden "cryptic" reality can be depicted only through a series of symbols, which evoke a "misty", obscure, mysterious atmosphere, one that can be detected in the art of Romanti-

cism and Decadence. The leading French Symbolist poets were Arthur Rimbaud, Stephane Mallarme, Paul Verlaine, and Charles Baudelaire.

Indeed, Baudelaire was the most prominent of the Symbolist poets. In 1857, he published his colossal work of poetry, entitled "Les Fleurs du Mal" ("The Flowers of Evil"). In 1886, the first periodical of Symbolist poetry was established, entitled "La Vogue."

Spirituality, imagination, sensuality, musicality, dream-like atmosphere, bewildering darkness, mysterious, hazy softness, a touch of decadence and melancholy—these are among the most prominent manifestations of Symbolist poetry. Symbolist poets

(mostly in France but also in Russia, Belgium, Germany, and England) were convinced that the only way in which a poet can portray internal reality and the psyche of human beings is by employing a series of symbols. Those symbols, once deciphered, are associated with emotionality, sensuality, musicality, and ramified associations. For this very reason, Symbolist poets rejected not only Realism and Naturalism, but also Impressionism.

Those three schools of art (Naturalism and Realism in literature and Impressionism in painting) strove to depict daily reality in the most accurate and precise fashion. Symbolist poets, on the other hand, were looking for the absolute truth, the hidden truth behind the mundane, realistic truth, truth that can be exposed and appreciated only by creating a series of symbols, which evoke associations and create an aura of mysticism.

According to the Symbolist poets, only a sequence of symbols and images can lead us to expose and fathom the hidden, absolute truth of poetry. The obscure, mysterious, profound attributes of Symbolist poetry also stem from the combination of elements of concrete reality and their counterparts of fantasy, myth, legend, and dream. The latter aspects are further reinforced by the lack of specificity of the historical/social context in which the poem is anchored. Also, while in Naturalism and Realism the

depicted reality is portrayed as a sequence, an evolution of social and historical events, Symbolist poetry
presents images and situations in a still, "frozen,"
"spatial" state. The Symbolist poem delivers an
opaque impression, one that is generated by dream,
or by illusion.

Furthermore, the Symbolist poem introduces a
unity, which is based on contradictions, on a paradoxical reality, one that contains no realistic connections to bridge the various components of the text.

The Symbolist poem also draws unexpected
analogies between sensual, sexual experiences and
celestial, sacred, spiritual, or divine experiences.

The language of the Symbolist poem evokes musical sensuality, much more intense than the customary musicality of the traditional language of poetic texts.

In this respect, the poetry of Edith Covensky displays distinct aesthetic characteristics associated with Symbolist poetry. One can trace in her poems a sequence of colorful images, associations, metaphors, symbols, statements, and metonyms which serve as a gate through which an attentive sensitive reader can pass in his/her quest for the hidden enigmatic meanings of the text, and discover the profound philosophy, the absolute truth.

Like many Symbolist poets, Edith Covensky's poems foster a certain mystique, an obscure inscrutable atmosphere, one that intimates a hidden, quintessential rather than concrete and mundane reality. Symbolist poetry addresses the senses, not necessarily empirical logic. Like Symbolist poetry, where the musicality and sensuality of the text are of paramount importance, Covensky's poetry, too, strives to orchestrate the sounds of the words into a rich sensual texture.

The following poems are examples of French Symbolist poetry. They are followed by several Symbolist-like poems by Edith Covensky.

CORRESPONDENCES
(Charles Beaudelaire)

Nature is a temple, lines of living signs
Sometimes uttering confused words;
A man is going through forests of symbols
Gazing at him with well known eyes.

And like echoes mixing in the remote distance
In one combination, obscure and abyss-like,
As vast as the night and like the encircling light

Colors, sounds , perfumes , they
    reciprocally correspond.
There is fresh perfume, as fresh as
    the flesh of a baby,
As sweet as an oboe, as green as the prairie,
And also: corrupt, celebrating and rich
    – bountiful scents ,
Expanding like endless things
Like incense, amber, myrrh, rot ,
Chanting enthusiastically of spirit and senses.

Source: William Aggeler, *The Flowers of Evil*
(Fresno, CA: Academy Library Guild, 1954)]

This poem demonstrates the aesthetic qualities of Symbolist poetry, which is echoed by that of Edith Covensky.

TO A CREOLE LADY

In a perfumed land , caressed by the sun,
I recognized, among trees dipped in crimson,
And palm trees embody laziness on the eyes,
A mulatto woman, her unknown
 spellbinding charm.

Her color is pale and warm, brown magician
Holding on her neck noble air;
She is tall and sublime, stepping like a hunter,
Her smile is serene, her eyes are confident.

Had you brought, my lady, to the land of glory,
To the banks of the Seine or to the Loire Valley,
The splendor of your beauty that
 can decorate ancient palaces

You were sowing among the shadowy
 hiding places
Thousands of sonnets in the hearts of the poets,
Your eyes may enslave then like the black lads.

Source: William Aggeler, *The Flowers of Evil*
(Fresno, CA: Academy Library Guild, 1954)]

Below is a cluster of poems by Edith Covensky that reflect Symbolist characteristics, such as lack of causality or apparent logic, temporal connections among the components of the poem, as well as a certain mysterious atmosphere and mellow and fluid musicality. However, the absence of apparent logic in the structure of the poem should not deceive us. In both Symbolist poetry and in Edith Covensky's poetry, that absence is replaced by other, subtler connections, which create their own unity in accordance with their own internal hidden logic.

Moreover, Covensky's poetry echoes Symbolist poetry by creating an aura of sensuality and musicality through associations, themes, images, metaphors, and sounds.

The following Symbolist-inspired examples from Edith Covensky's poetry demonstrate and underline the existence of latent integrating links. They include sensual experiences, colorful, enigmatic images, a touch of mystery, and unexpected transitions from one poetic unit (image, metaphor, metonym, expression, association, statement) to the next, as well a strong musical, euphonious element.

As in Symbolist poetry, Covensky's poems are replete with ramified, dense clusters of associations. Thus, these poems testify to the manifold aesthetic ties connecting her poetry to the Symbolist movement (while her connection to Futurism and Stream of Consciousness are more tenuous).

Arie Menes, Composition #03031401 ©

TESTIMONY

My eyes quiver drunkenly
Bear my loneliness like a scarlet bird
Silent among the droplets of darkness .

My time is entwined in the poem
Like the testimony of the poet
And as a silent promise
Spinning magic.

I am a woman of dreams:
My light is shadow
A fictitious sun embroiders my words
Scented in flight
Open to love.

WORDS BINDING WORDS

My puzzle poem is clarified in festivity
Drawn to the sun in concentrated intensity
Gust in Deception
Nobly mobilized in tune.

And I am like a shore bird
Gliding in this optimism
Grayish aware of the light
Shaking free in my flight.

And the words bind words
In an enthusiastic scheme revealing my song
Devised in me in summer.

GEOLOGICAL SAND

I am a desert rover
Confused amidst fire burned substances
And geological sand
And savage bird sounds

I play on a hot yellow ground
And my eyes blaze amidst the shadows
Whispering conciliatory words
With a roar gleaming in me
Spread out like in an open field.

The night covers my body
Rotating in childishly covered silence
Rolling in a main street

There I wander naked among the sea shells.

CYCLICAL LOVE

My love is made from my cycle of poems
And from the recommended conciliation
And from the quotidian dreams.

And I adorn myself with a musical painting
Folded within me
Between words
Playing peacefully almost like God.

I find nothing here except the sun
Tepid in a bedecked optimistic tale
Enchanting in its confusion.

I even have young primitive bubbling words
Refined by light
Intimate on the first pages
In order to extract from me
In order to fly.

I AM SILENT AS A FLOWER

My love hot in the midst of illusion
Lifts off in splendor among lucid memories
Washing over my window.

And children play among flowers
Entwined within loneliness
Blushing at sunset
Shaking themselves off at dawn.

I am silent as a flower
Created in light engulfing me
Glowing in my path
Roaring with a smile
Falling silent.

I PAINT A SUN

I paint a sun
A fantasy in the spirit of time
A deafening illusion I have to escape from
Coupled with me
Charisma strengthening in my memory
Hallucinating dabbling in magic.

There is actually here the very
*   making of the poem*
A woman seeking love on a mad day
Crouching between the lines
With limpid desire
Like a flower in the abundance of light.

METAPHYSICS

I am attached to the sea
Adore the sun
The limits are unclear to me.

My language is a flower
A wave of light gathering in my head
Also revealed in the days to come.

And my desiring eyes spark in soft gladness
And in multicolored dreams
And in optimistic stars.

My words are so muddled
My memories reconcile among tall trees
As if they touch my body
As if they hurt.

ORIENTAL LAMENTATION

My dream is drawn in free rhythm
Mixed with alchemy
Whirling among streets and sand
Clothed in sad beauty.

The music is desire and sadness
Floating like an oriental lamentation
Among rare flowers.

What feeling appeases me
My laughter is drunken
My body wanders exiled

This is possible only thanks to the wind.

IN THE CRADLE OF POETRY

I depend on the pranks of time
My voice echoes with longing
My love invents your being.

My hand clasps your mysteries
Trembles with a new vision
My wintery day wanders
Rocking in the cradle of your song.

And the words shatter in nothingness
Flower from my thought at sunset
Crouch on my lips
Mingle with the wind.

As noted previously, the third literary school from which the poetry of Edith Covensky seems to draw inspiration is Stream of Consciousness in prose fiction. We saw earlier that in the case of Symbolist poetry, the similarity consists in multilayered, intricate affinities. Whereas in the case of Futurist poetry, the resemblance of Edith Covensky's poetry to it is limited to the lack of causality and temporality, in the case of Stream of Consciousness the resemblance is considerably more substantial.

The term 'Stream of Consciousness' was coined by William James in his book, *The Principles of Psychology* (1890). In literature (prose fiction, mostly novels but also short stories) the term refers to works of literature in which the traditional "external" plot is replaced by an internal plot; the flowing stream of thoughts consists of associations (which are founded on either metaphors or metonyms or on both), feelings, wishes, recollections, ideas, and more. All of these are conveyed and filtered through the consciousness of a character, be it the main protagonist or a marginal character.

In this respect, the literary mode of Stream of Consciousness corresponds to the psychological novel (sometimes called lyrical novel), which takes as its subject matter the uninterrupted, erratic flow of "internal monologues" by the fictional character.

Thus, in a Stream of Consciousness work, the causal, logical, rational, temporal or developmental connections among the textual units (words, phrases, sentences, paragraphs, chapters) are replaced by ongoing internal monologue/s that reflect the internal emotional and mental life of the character/s. In this respect, the prose fiction of Stream of Consciousness establishes "spatial" links (in contradistinction to developmental, temporal, and causal connections) among the various components of the text.

Thus, the main literary tool employed by a Stream of Consciousness novel/story is the pre-speech, non-verbal, unarticulated experiences and states of mind (either concrete or psychological and emotional), and the manner in which they are experienced and expressed by the character's consciousness.

Among the leading authors of Stream of Consciousness are James Joyce, William Faulkner, Virginia Woolf, Henry James, Marcel Proust, Knut Hamsun (the novels *Mysteries*" and *Hunger*), and Anton Chekhov in some of his short stories.

Undoubtedly, the most prominent example of Stream of Consciousness is *Ulysses*, by James Joyce. The following section—Molly Bloom's internal monologue—exemplifies the literary nature of Stream of Consciousness.

"A quarter after what an unearthly hour I
suppose they're just getting up in China now
combing out their pigtails for the day will soon
have the suns ringing the angelus they've
nobody is coming to spoil their sleep except an
odd priest or two for his night office or the alarm-
clock next door cock-shout clattering the brain
out of itself let me see if I can doze of 12345
what kind of flowers are those they invented like
the stars of wallpaper in Lombard street was
much nicer the apron he gave me was like that
something only I only wore it twice better lower
this lamp and try again so that I can get up
early...."

The following poems by Edith Covensky seem to reflect the basic tenets of Stream of Consciousness, where the traditional, causal, temporal, developmental and logical connections among the textual units are removed, and are replaced by connections consisting of "spatial", internal associations, analogies, thoughts, and feelings.

A LOCAL FLOWER

I am drunk
Quaking among shards of identities
Of winter
Of summer

Mute hour after hour
As in a silent picture from an old movie.

Your shadow is revealed
Looking like a walk that expands you
        on all sides
Gaining time
Saying things quickly
Among local flowers
Bound to a single geographic center.

Here time builds time
As though repeating for me the count of hours.

ANOTHER POEM FOR VAN GOGH

You move among crowded matter
Cross through my dreams with symbolic words
Like flowers in a yellow vase.

Your language is alive
Your love wraps itself in night
Like a quick painting of a melting tear.

This rain is different
Breaking in quick time
Aligned with objects torn from my desire
Entangled on paper such as this
In laughable tension.

SUMMER FLOWERS

I dive into the whites of your eyes
In exact trembling light
Inventing a myth for myself.

This comes to me directly from summer flowers
In a night disappearing from the street
Among lilies broken in hidden tension.

What is all this poetic compression
Gathering in a new version
Drawn outside of time.

The metaphor is complete
Playing among my pleasures
Grasped like possible illusion.

A STAR IN JERUSALEM

Jerusalem is tumultuous in silence
Waved aloft crowded in the landscape
Bound bursting before me
In an illusory colorful text.

I ponder the stone
Silent in thought
Overturned in the thicket of old-fashioned speech
Still-life
Like a star in Jerusalem
Vibrant at dawn.

And I grow dizzy in purity
Among memories hinting at a great yearning
Whispering words in heaven.

SEA LILY

My love merges in me
Between words
Seduced with gaiety
Embracing in tumult.

My longings are painted beauty
In childishness retreating to the poem
Among vibrant lines
Out of great excitement.

My musicality gathers among the sea lilies
Devolves among symbols
Sparks flow on these pages
In light addicted to illusion.

And the sun is a colorful fiction
Setting fleeting sketch
Mute in the great uproar.

FOR ELSA LASKER SCHULER

I fold my love
Among bundles of mute pages
A pearl gleaming with great excitement.

It is hard for me to resist this temptation
A cosmopolitan flier
Like a swallow taking off in silence.

And you steal into the vision
Invade me with a funny whisper
Pressed on a wrinkled page
Tempt like a nocturnal lover.

What longing is renewed in the poem
A flying bird tangled in haste
Broken in the current
Facing an embarrassed tear.

I TELL ABOUT CHEKHOV

I see a sun in this place
Touch you with my words
Enchanted bound within me
Among colors tempered with luster.

I also tell of Chekhov in the summer
Tossing among memories against a clear portrait
Revealing my weakness
Entangled in strong desire.

My thought wonders these days
Grows clear confused in confession
Uncovers my fears at night
Like a camera preserving things.

And then I play in my dreams
Invert stars with great speed
Fly like a daughter of God.

TEMPTATIONS

I write confession after confession
Revealing temptations stubbornly
Laughing on a wet day
Among shadows clear in the landscape.

I become popular
Sing like a night bird
Crowded lively in illusion
Living as though bestowing beauty on things.

I do not deny my deceptions
Touch the slate of my memory
With a reflection like a poem
Between words yellowing in the sun.

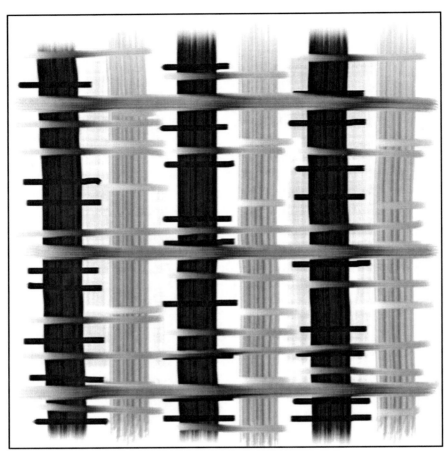

Arie Menes, Composition #03031404-2 ©

BEHIND THE POETIC CURTAIN: HOW TO READ EDITH COVENSKY'S POETRY

Erupting in a storm of words
On a public bench
And writing again on the sand
What the sea will not erase.
(Edith Covensky)

This chapter aims to introduce and analyze leading aesthetic trends and characteristics in Edith Covenky's poetry. It exposes and examines the poetic mechanism by which aesthetic devices help us decode the "cryptic message" embedded in the poems.

TECTONIC FRACTURE

I conscript my love
Like a marine archeologist
A diver amidst tectonic fractures
Murmuring nostalgically
Simple silent words.

And my pain
Confuses things
Revolving to the middle of the poem
Feeble in the shadows
Like words breaking in water.

My night is extinguished
      among a thousand sparks.

The poem opens with a declaration by the lyrical narrator [like all poems by Edith Covensky, the poem's narrator is a first-person lyrical speaker/ narrator] that she "conscripts her love." For what purpose? For composing her poetry.

However, the next lines clearly show that love— even ardent, fervent love—is not sufficient for the composition of her poetry. The process of composing poetry—the lyrical speaker asserts - not only involves and requires love, but it is also a demanding, challenging, and painful process. These sentiments are like a quarry from which the poet carves her poems.

The first stanza of the poem portrays through metaphors the subtle process of composing a poem. The metaphorical image of "tectonic fractures" conveys the challenging, demanding task that confronts the poet while composing her poetry.

The water motif joins together the two stanzas. In the first stanza, we read about "marine archeologist," and in the second stanza, we read about "words breaking in water." This way, the poem introduces an

integrating link that negates the first confusing impression of having two stanzas that seem utterly detached and removed from each other.

However, the poem's unity is obtained through an even more intricate system of affinities between the two stanzas.

According to the second stanza, the process of composing poetry is not only challenging and demanding, but also painful. Moreover, the "confused things" that "revolve to the middle of the poem" are "feeble," as they are anchored "in the shadows." Thus, while a "marine archeologist" (in the first stanza) must be exceedingly careful while unearthing ancient archeological relics that have been buried in the sea for thousands of years (and are therefore "feeble," i.e., fragile), the pain and the "things" (poetic components) in the second stanza are as feeble and fragile as words that break down in water. Thus, even after confronting the challenging, demanding nature of the process of composing poetry, the process is still very fragile, like the archeological relics retrieved from the depth of the sea.

Another element integrating the two stanzas of the poem is the following: while the first stanza ends with a reference to feeble words (the feeble/fragile poem), the second stanza also ends with a reference to fragile, feeble words ("like words breaking in water").

The poem ends with the verse: "My night is extinguished among a thousand sparks."

The verb "extinguished" echoes effectively the feeble nature of the poem's words, so feeble that they are as fragile as archeological relics found at the bottom of the sea. This way, the concluding line of the poem further "weaves" one more integrating link between the two stanzas.

Furthermore, the final words of the poem, "a thousand sparks," endow the poem with a cosmic dimension, which derives from the "prophetic" vision of the cosmic creation, one that produced "thousand sparks." This way, the poem is elevated from an earthly level to a cosmic level.

This poem is about the painful demanding process of writing poetry, a process which yields feeble/ fragile results (poems), as fragile as archeological relics lodged at the bottom of the sea (first stanza), as fragile as the words of the poems (second stanza).

However, the poem ends with a paradox: the night which is extinguished, thus creating darkness, also yields a thousand sparks of blinding light. This paradox symbolizes the very essence of the poem; the process of composing poetry is not only lofty, inspiring, captivating, but it is equally challenging, demanding, and even grueling.

This is a poem about a poem, about the art of composing poetry, a poem portraying *ars poetica*, the nature and essence of poetry, a poem about the elevated yet tormenting process of stringing words together and creating a poem. And love.

A CONFUSED DAY

My day twists with desire
Between hot words of summer
Revolving in a time of great pining.

I return to the poem
Playing childish games
Drawing a bird
And a flower turning into sound.

You amuse me with the tension
of a confused day
Floating from silence to silence
Remembered like a thought of night.

Like so many poems by Edith Covensky, this poem describes the process of composing a poem, the *ars poetica*, which is the aesthetic foundation of a poem.

Although the first line of the poem – "My day twists with desire" – seems to express the fervent feeling of the first-person lyrical narrator, the second line sheds a new light on the first line: "between hot words of summer." The narrator shifts the focus from her own ardent desire to her poem, which is conveyed through the phrase "hot words of summer." In fact, summer is the hot element here, yet the hot summer inspires the poem's words by making them hot as well.

The "hot words of summer" are "revolving in a time of great pining." Here, the process of creating a poem begins; the words, as hot as the summer, are undergoing metamorphosis as they experience "a time of great pining." The great pining of the hot words, which are as hot as summer (summer bestows its heat on the poetic words) forms part of the writing process. That pining guides the poem to its vortex.

In the second stanza, the lyrical narrator "returns to the poem." The process of composing the poem seems to have reached its culmination in the second stanza that introduces the poem as a complete entity. But here a surprise awaits the reader who has assumed that the poem is complete: his/her expectations—based on that assumption—are frustrated. (This is a neat rhetorical device of the poem's aesthetic mechanism.) Thus, the lyrical narrator does not only "return to the poem" (which seems to be complete) but she does so "playing childish games." That play brings to mind a new understanding that the poem is not complete yet.

Like the innocent perspective of a child who views the world for the first time, the lyrical narrator returns to being a child ("playing childish games/ drawing a bird"), adopting a child's perspective. Thus, the poem is not yet complete, since the process of its creation is still based on the perspective of a child, one only starting to face the world. That innocent, initial perspective is adopted by the poem's lyrical speaker/narrator. This reverts the poem to an inchoate, almost embryonic, state of existence.

The next verse introduces "a flower turning into sound." This is also part of the creative process. The beauty of the flower—a symbol of innocence that echoes a child's perspective – is "turning into sound." This is the sound of the budding poem, one that is no longer mute.

The third and last stanza opens thus: "You amuse me with a tension of a confused day."

Who is "you?" This unseen, silent addressee of the poem is possibly the unidentified reader of the poem. Although the "you" is mute and unseen, s/he has a role in creating and "sprouting" the poem.

Thus, that anonymous addressee of the poem amuses the lyrical narrator "with the tension of a confused day." The confused day is the day of composing the poem. That day is "confused" because the process of composing a poem is "bumpy" and "uneven," requiring weighing different options of writing and, therefore, it can be appropriately described as "confused." That confusion, however, explains the "tension" which is associated with the process of composing poetry. The unseen reader wishes to amuse the confused lyrical narrator (as confused as the process of composing the poem).

And yet this attempt is a futile one, doomed to failure. The process of composing a poem will continue to be considerably bumpy and uneven, and thus demanding; one that is not conducive to "amusement."

The "confused" day is "floating from silence to silence." Silence, muteness, is the state of the poem before its creation, before "turning into sound." Hence, the poem is still far from being complete, it is still in the rudimentary, embryonic state of existence.

The final line of the poem reads: "Remembered like a thought of night."

The poem is the one that is "remembered like a thought of night." The poem is not only far from being complete; the embryonic poem has not even begun to sprout.

In the first stanza of the poem, there is a reference to "summer." The final word of the poem is "night."

Since "summer" is associated with connotations of bright light, the poem reaches its culmination with "night." Dark, bleak night is the opposite of sunny, cheery "summer." Hence, the ending of the poem throws the reader back to the beginning of the poem, to the bright, summery light. This light will hopefully extricate the poem from its lightless state, and lead it to a state of "budding" and "blossoming." The latter further stresses the idea of the difficulty associated with composing a poem.

Moreover, the word "summer" in Hebrew is "*ka'itz*" which is etymologically connected to ending, termination ["*ketz*"]. Thus, one may cogently argue that the beginning of the poem with its summer reference foreshadows the ending of the poem with its reference to night, which also has a connotation of ending, termination, or awaiting a new beginning.

This short poem, then, with its first impression of illogicality, actually presents a kind of inner logic all its own, which is found in its depth. A close reading

Arie Menes, Composition #02261411 ©

of this poem unveils a profundity that makes it a very rewarding poetic experience.

This is also an *ars poetica* poem (like so many poems by Edith Covensky), one that describes the rough and uneven road that leads to the composing of even a single poem.

The following observation is relevant to all works of literature (poetry in this case). The literary text is conceived and presented by an "implied author" (following Wayne Booth's definition). All the components of the work, aesthetic devices, literary inclinations, meaning, "message," and all other aspects associated with the literary text—are the results of the way in which the "implied author" of the text (who is abstract) plans, shapes, conceives, constructs and orchestrates the text.

The lyrical narrator/speaker is a rhetorical device (created by the "implied author") through his/her perspective; the literary text communicates with the reader. All those theoretical observations about the way the literary text operates should guide the reader toward a critical approach in both poetry and prose fiction (drama is the only literary genre that has no narrator/speaker).

AN ILLUSION ASSAILS ME

An illusion assails me
Revealed hidden in words
Sophisticated in a monograph of this kind.

I explode the night
In some attractive seductive inspiration
Connected to a great love.

My weakness is central
Uncoiling in a quick limber language
As if slipping amongst the rituals.

And then I insinuate into rhyme
Amused by imaginary desires
Drawing another poem
With sensitive pencil.

This poem continues to explore the leading theme of Edith Covensky's poetry: composing *ars poetica* poems that depict the painful yet gratifying process of composing poetry. Indeed, documenting *ars poetica*, studying the complicated yet rewarding process of composing poetry, is probably one of the most distinctive leitmotifs in the poetry by Edith Covensky.

The poem opens with the verses:

"An illusion assails me
Revealed hidden in words
Sophisticated in a monograph of this kind."

The fact that the lyrical first-person speaker reports an illusion that has attacked her may be interpreted as follows: the illusion is, in fact, the essence of poetry (and of art in general), since an illusion is based on fiction which is the opposite of concrete, empirical, reality. The poet and her poem are "doomed" to lag behind the colorful, teeming reality that the poem aims to portray. Hence, concrete reality always promises a protective shelter, which the art of poetry (and other arts as well) cannot offer.

The fact that the lyrical narrator is assailed by an illusion reveals the following: the lyrical narrator "enlists" all her aesthetic faculties in order to prevent, or at least by-pass, the collapse of that illusion. After all, illusion and fiction are the essential materials of various kinds of art. Nevertheless, like all illusions,

the poetic illusion in this poem eventually collapses under the "yoke" of sober-minded reality. That is the eternal paradox of all art: art—in all mediums—is based on illusion, on fiction that purports to portray reality but at the same time wishes to create its own fictional, alluring reality.

Thus, the illusion in the first stanza is both revealed and hidden in words. The "hidden" part of this equation is the attempt – which is doomed to fail —to adopt that illusion, while pretending that it is concrete reality. The "revealed" part of that equation is the process of sobering up from that artistic illusion, from its nature that leads astray.

The final line of the first stanza reads: "Sophisticated in a monograph of this kind."

A monograph in a literary context is a scholarly composition. In the case of this poem, even a "sophisticated" monograph is doomed to fail in the vain attempt to overcome or avoid the outcome of the eventual collapse of the illusion, an illusion challenged by concrete, earthly reality.

The lyrical narrator continues her monologue:

"I explode the night
In some attractive seductive inspiration
Connected to a great love."

Both "night" and "love" are among the most common and powerful motifs in Edith Covensky's poetry. Yet, in each poem that employs these motifs, they are wrought according to the specific "recipe" of the particular poem. In this poem, the lyrical speaker attacks (by exploding) the night while being armed with an "attractive seductive inspiration," which is "connected to a great love."

Indeed, the lyrical narrator echoes the way in which an illusion operates; while the illusion attacks ("assails") the lyrical narrator, the creator of fiction (created and operated by the "implied author, rhetorically represented by the lyrical narrator), the lyrical narrator attacks ("explodes") the night. Her failure can be easily predicted by the illusion (in its current disguise as "night" that will eventually prevail).

The inspiration that guides and impels the lyrical narrator to attack the night, is of an "attractive seductive" nature, one that is "connected to a great love." Thus, the attack on the night by the lyrical narrator is fraught with alluring beauty ("attractive seductive") and "love." Yet even the alluring beauty, the seductive inspiration and love are, regrettably (from the subjective point of view of the lyrical narrator) not sufficient weapons to overcome the illusion. Thus the illusion will always be inferior to the concrete reality, which is poetically portrayed.

Thus, directly and indirectly, the first two stanzas

address the illusive issue in the context of poetry, in the process of composing poetry. Attacking, exploding the night, even while armed with love, seduction, and inspiration, is doomed to failure. The power of the illusion, the shielding protection of the poem (both revealed and hidden words, according to the first stanza) will eventually collapse under the burden of "real" empirical reality. Thus, the power of the illusion equals the power of the poem—the poem is illusive since it is not made of concrete, empirical reality— and will eventually succumb to superior, concrete reality.

The process of creating poetry may put poetry on a very high pedestal, but at the end of the day, the poetically portrayed earthly, concrete reality will prevail. To be sure, this does not diminish the value of the poetically portrayed poem. Nevertheless, the above-mentioned recognition puts things in a realistic perspective. And the poet is caught between his/her wish to extol poetry and the realistic limitation of poetry.

> "My weakness is central
> Uncoiling in a quick limber language
> As if slipping amongst the rituals"

In spite of the fact that the language of the lyrical narrator is "a quick limber language," agile and skillful enough to "slip amongst the rituals," it cannot make up for the inability of the lyrical narrator to convert it into victory. Reality is always more robust and prominent than poetic fiction. Hence, the poet is defeated by the poetic attempt to create a poem, on the one hand, and by the weak nature of poetry (compared to concrete reality) on the other.

> "And then I insinuate into rhyme
> Amused by imaginary desires
> Drawing another poem
> With sensitive pencil."

The lyrical narrator is struggling while engaged in the process of producing a poem ("And then I insinuate into rhyme"). She also permits herself to be "amused by imaginary chains/rings," meaning illusive material, since the chains are only imaginary. This is the essence of composing poetry; it enables the lyrical narrator "to draw another poem/ With a sensitive pencil."

Thus the process of composing the poem has finally come to an end. Now it is time for "another poem" to speak out.

I AM ALMOST NONEXISTENT

I apologize from the very first line of the poem
Playing among the words
Against descendent stars creating the night.

And I am tempted from page to page
Among broken illusions
Flowing in time
Like sand
And sun on the living flesh.

And the poem corrects the day for me
Liquid in memory like water
Rolling tranquilly in the wind.

I am almost nonexistent.

The poem opens with the statement: "I apologize from the very first line of the poem"

Why does the lyrical narrator beg for forgiveness? The only way to answer this question is by realizing that the lyrical narrator includes the reader in the detailed process of creating the poem, and does not just present the reader with the final product, the completed poem. The process of creating a poem is long, detailed, and demanding; it is a rough and bumpy road.

The narrator appears to be dedicated to the truth, the truth of narrating the entire process of composition; she does not wish to ignore or avoid that truth.

The process of composing the poem is carried out by "playing among the words." Hence, this is the start of creating and molding the poem; the lyrical narrator is still playing among the words, not sure yet which ones she will select to be included in the poem.

"Against descendent stars creating the night."

The stars are "bowing" to the night, which they create. The allusion to Joseph's dream in Genesis, in which all his family bows to him, is quite evident. In both texts it is nighttime, and there are stars in the sky. Like the humble pardon, which the lyrical narrator begs in the first line of the poem, the bowing ("descendent") stars exhibit similar meekness.

The stars create the night as God created light from the void. This juxtaposition of light and night underlines the metaphorical process of creating a poem; after a flurry of activity, which takes place in the dark, the poem, the light, is born.

"And I am tempted from page to page
Among broken illusions
Flowing in time
Like sand
And sun on living flesh."

The lyrical narrator, the "rhetorical speaker" of the poem, is tempted to introduce the reader only to the final result of the slow process of creating the poem. The image of the poet flipping pages corroborates the earlier statement; to be or not to be, to introduce or not to introduce the reader to the entire process of creating the poem, not just the final result of that lengthy process, i.e., the poem per se. Here is the proof:

"Among broken illusions
Flowing in time
Like sand
And sun on living flesh."

The illusions that pave the long road of creation prove to be vain and idle. The ardent expectations are broken and frustrated, and time goes on obliviously, paying no heed to the narrator's chagrin, flowing imperturbably like sand in an hourglass.

Traditionally, the sun is associated with positive qualities such as warmth, openness to the world, life, creation, bright light, etc. However, the sun may also be associated with scorching heat, drought, and arid, lifeless deserts. Those negative connotations of the sun are here enlisted by the lyrical narrator to describe the harshness of the creative process.

"And the poem corrects the day for me
Liquid in memory like water
Rolling tranquilly in the wind."

The poem "corrects the day" for the lyrical narrator; this is the way the poem compensates for the toil and pain that the narrator endured before and while begetting the poem.

From now on, the lyrical narrator's experience is dramatically improved; her memory is as gentle as water streaming peacefully, rolling tranquilly in the tender, caressing wind.

In this poem, the lyrical narrator introduces an equation between the lyrical narrator and her poem. She goes through excruciating pain to "give birth" to the poem and the poem generously reciprocates by bestowing on her serenity and tenderness.

The poem ends with the line: "I am almost non-existent."

Once her task—the creation of a poem—has been fulfilled in a rewarding fashion, once her presence is no longer required, she can step down from the creative post and retire. This may sound cruel but, perhaps, it is in accord with the wishes of the lyrical narrator herself. For once her mission is accomplished, it is time for her to retire, to rest, to step down from her post and take her leave. The poem has now to assume its own task, fulfill its own role.

A BALLAD

I am born from the poem's breath
Looking for identity in sound filled things
Revealing myself
Twisted in a kind of delusion.

And the sea silences my voice
Playing with still words
Revolving across the puzzle of night
Folding up amid the gusts of wind
And the illusion of my lips
In a sea of signs flowing in such absurdity.

I insist on existing between a living day
and its collapse.

The poem opens with a paradox. In most poetic instances, the "implied author" is represented by the lyrical narrator (the rhetorical vehicle used by the "implied author"), the one that creates the poem. In this poem, however, the lyrical narrator is the one who is "born from the poem's breath."

This paradox, in which the poem and the lyrical narrator exchange roles, underlines the closeness between the lyrical narrator and her poem. However, that paradox in which the lyrical narrator loses her original identity causes the narrator to look "for identity in sound filled things." The sound, which is filled with "things," is indeed the poem, the one whose sound and things are put before the reader. Here is another paradox; while in a traditional poetic literary text, the latter is the one associated with exposing identity, in this poem the lyrical narrator is the one who is looking for identity.

The fact that the lyrical narrator and her poem exchange roles underlines the tight closeness between her and the poem. Thus the earthly "thing" (the lyrical narrator) and the other "thing" (the poem) are firmly connected to each other.

As for the part of the lyrical narrator, that process in which her identity becomes obscure (who is she? herself or the poem?) is confusing and compels the lyrical narrator to reveal herself. As her identity is exposed, the confusion disappears. The lyrical narrator is also "twisted in a kind of delusion." And yet, she informs the reader that despite her quest for the "lost" identity, her true identity is still quite elusive and enigmatic.

The second stanza continues the narrator's focus on the quest for her true identity. However, this mission proves a challenging one; the sea silences her voice; it plays with still words that are her opaque poetic faculties.

Those still words are the poem:

"[words of the poem] are revolving across the puzzle of night
Folding up amid the gusts of wind..."

All those chronicles of the still words, the words of the poem, are not sufficient to unveil the true identity of the lyrical narrator. Hence, the night is still a confusing puzzle; the words are still and mute, unequal to their true mission to speak out. Those words confront in vain the gusts of wind, which fold the words. The lips of the lyrical narrator are her still, mute words. Those words are an illusion—unlike the true task of lips—since they are the verbalized poem, they are the vocally uttered poem. All those experiences and chronicles are stumbling blocks making the lyrical narrator's mission—to find her true identity— almost impossible.

....."And the illusion of my lips
In a sea of signs flowing in such absurdity."

Again, the illusion, the stumbling block on the way to unmasking that illusion, to reveal its internal identity, cannot provide the needed clue that will enable the lyrical narrator to unveil her true identity. Her lips, her vocally expressed words, are still vague. The illusion is still a major obstacle to finding her true identity, which is still surrounded by the "sea of signs flowing in such absurdity."

Indeed, a poem may be metaphorically portrayed as a sea of signs, since the language of the poem (like any other language) consists of signs that the target audience (the readers of the poem) is expected to decode and decipher. Those signs are fraught with "such absurdity" that it is one more stumbling block on the way to revealing the hidden, true identity of the narrator.

Since an absurdity cannot make sense as the true identity of the lyrical narrator, it seems to be doomed to remain devoid of sense. Hence, the poet's desire to unlock her true identity remains vague, obscure, and as confusing as ever. The lyrical narrator will never be able to overcome such overwhelming obstacles. Her true identity will remain a haunting, ambiguous mystery.

"I insist on existing between a living day and its collapse."

These are two existential states of mind that the narrator confronts on her unsuccessful way to find her true identity. However, the gulf between those two different states of mind is dangerously narrow, causing the lyrical narrator to confuse them. Yet she insists on living on such a perilous line between a "living day and its collapse." Perhaps, her true identity is placed somewhere between those two entities. Or maybe not. The lyrical narrator leaves us with a question mark, an unresolved confusion. The true identity of the lyrical narrator will remain an enigma.

Like so many poems by Edith Covensky, this poem is also an *ars poetica* poem, a poem that addresses the aesthetic process of conceiving and begetting poetry. In this case, however, the true identity of the lyrical narrator, the one that should expose the mysterious nature of the poem, remains as enigmatic as ever.

There is a saying in the *Mishna* (the code of oral Jewish law): "No man leaves this world with even half his wishes fulfilled." The wish to reveal the true identity of the lyrical narrator, the true identity of her poem, will remain unfulfilled.

I AM A REVOLUTIONARY

I am a revolutionary turning stars
Circling in the secret of night
Drawing illusion with illusion.

And the poem has a chance
Rising in the grace of day
In a giddy play
Bound on paper.

In fact, I have no other pleasure
Singing among the strings of my love
Wrapped in words born in me
Like a flower renewed in silence.

This poem, too, focuses on *ars poetica*, the process of conceiving and creating poetry. This theme will be discussed and amplified through the analysis of the poem.

The poem opens with the statement:

"I am a revolutionary turning stars

Circling in the secret of night
Drawing illusion with illusion."

A revolutionary is a person who is ardently devoted to an idea, such as equality among all people, freedom to practice one's religion, freedom of speech, free press, etc. A revolutionary typically rejects old traditions, which do not correspond to his/her own ideas, or ideas that were held before the new ones were conceived. A revolutionary desires to introduce a new agenda or a set of beliefs, unorthodox ideas and credo, with a view to improving the lives of people in society.

In this poem, however, the revolutionary is very ambitious: she considers herself the chosen one who can turn stars in their celestial orbits, to "circle in the secret of the night."

The third line of the first stanza casts a new light on the revolutionary's lofty ambition. The nature of the new revolution is nothing but "illusion with illusion." As in most works of literature, the leading trend consists of tension, of lack of congruence, between the early information introduced along the accumulative textual continuum and later information.

The later information may just add to the previous, early information, or it may introduce altogether new material that forces the reader to reverse the earlier reading and update the way in which he/she interpreted the early information. The most crucial stage in this dynamic of the literary text is the way later information casts dramatic new light on the early information; the reader is forced to practice reverse reading, to return to the early information, and replace the way in which the early information was previously understood with a dramatically different, new understanding.

in a nutshell, this is the nature of literary dynamics; it can be realized only due to the accumulative, "horizontal" nature of the literary text, in which there is always a reciprocal dialogue between early information and later information. That process does not allow for a direct, linear experience of reading, offering instead a "bumpy," circuitous reading experience.

This is the drama of reading, which consists of perennial tension between early information and later information. In the first stanza of the poem, the later information ("drawing illusion with illusion") casts new light on the "cosmic" revolution of the lyrical narrator, presented earlier (she turns heavenly stars, she encircles in the secret of the night, which alludes to the creation of the world in the book of Genesis). Hence, the first, early impression that portrays the lyrical narrator as a cosmic creator is found to be a false one; the lyrical narrator is besieged by her own, misleading, arrogant self-image.

> "And the poem has a chance
> Rising in the grace of day
> In a giddy play
> Bound on paper."

Although it turns out that the lyrical narrator is not a celestial creator, she is still an earthly creator, a creator of poetry. And her poem still has a chance to rise in a gracious, compassionate day. That elevation of the poem is indeed "a giddy play / bound on paper." The elevated poem is indeed "a giddy play" by a giddy poem that is "bound on paper." This added

information casts a new light on the earlier information, which has the reader doing reverse reading,
reading the poem backwards, in order to reinterpret
the early information in light of the newly provided
information along the textual continuum.

In this case, the later information—"bound on
paper"—enables the reader to comprehend more
accurately the real role and significance of the poem.
Thus, despite her lofty ambition to be a sublime,
cosmic creator, like the heavenly creator, at the end
of the day, her poem is not more elevated than a piece
of paper, in which it is bound.

"In fact I have no other pleasure
Signing among the strings of my love
Wrapped in words born in me
Like a flower renewed in silence."

In this third and final stanza, the lyrical narrator
shifts from focusing on the poem to focusing on
herself, the creator of the poem. According to her own
testimony, composing poetry of love, one that is
wrapped in the words created by the narrator, is her
only pleasure.

Moreover, she metaphorically portrays herself as a
flower, which is "renewed in silence." Here, the lyrical
narrator goes through a humbling metamorphosis;
she starts the poem as a haughty revolutionary, who

argues that she can turn the stars in their heavenly orbits, and she ends the poem with a more modest, humble cluster of words that can be compared to one single flower budding in silence. Concluding the poem with silence highlights the previous image of a poet whose uttered words can turn the celestial stars in their orbits.

Thus, the progression of the poem guides the reader's process of reading and comprehension, which oscillates between two aesthetic poles: the initial arrogant self-image of the proud revolutionary and her later humbler, meeker self image. This is the *ars poetica* of the poem; this is the art of reading literature: the drama inherent in any kind of text.

NIGHT WHISPER

My words are open to the wind
Rolling at eye level
Breaking like clay
In the void of time
And the shadow of water.

And love bursts out onto the whiteness
of the page
Becoming in the womb of my poem
Hiding objects on the grass
In the tonality of a soul living in great stillness
Trembling like God
Joining the whisper of the night.

Like so many poems of Edith Covensky, this poem introduces its own version of *ars poetica*, the process of creating poetry.

The first stanza of the poem reads:

"My words are open to the wind
Rolling at eye level
Breaking like clay
In the void of time
And the shadow of water.

Combining in one stanza both wind and water seems to echo the beginning of creation in the book of Genesis: ....." And the wind [spirit] of God was hovering over the water." Also, in the same stanza, there is a reference to "void" (in Biblical Hebrew "te'hom"), which brings to mind the darkness over

"te'hom" at the opening of the book of Genesis. The poem also alludes to "night" and "shadow," which seem to echo the darkness in Genesis, prior to the creation of light.

The expression "shadow of water" also seems to allude to the "darkness over the water" in the book of Genesis. By the same token, the "great stillness" in the poem echoes the absolute silence that prevailed during the creation of the world. The stillness in the poem also echoes the absolute universal stillness that descended on the world when the Israelites received the Torah from the hands of Moses at Mount Sinai [according to commentary by Talmudic sages].

The act of creating poetry is presented here as "becoming in the womb of my poem": "creation" is as profound as giving birth, as creating life, as the Biblical creation in Genesis.

Moreover, the poem ends with a "soul living," which brings to mind the following: When Adam/man is instructed by God to give names to all animals, it is said that every animal named by Adam would turn into "*nefesh Haiah*," "a living soul." This, again, is a clear reference to creation (in this case verbal creation) that may be metaphorically associated with creating poetry. In the Bible, the act of naming is a verbal means of creation. By naming the animals, they become "living souls"; when the patriarch Abram is renamed Abraham, when Sarai is renamed Sarah, and when Jacob is renamed Israel, all of them are spiritually elevated, re-created, through the act of renaming.

The allusions to the book of Genesis are further developed in the poem. The phrase "breaking like clay" reminds us of Adam, and subsequently all humanity, who were created from earth, from clay.

Arie Menes, Composition #05041304 ©

Thus, the numerous instances in the poem alluding to the creation in the book of Genesis, relate metaphorically to the act of creating the poem by the "implied author" through the rhetorical mediator, the lyrical narrator.

Since the poem opens with "My words are open to the wind," it seems to conflate the creation of the poem and the creation of the world in the book of Genesis ("*ru'akh*" in Biblical Hebrew is both wind and spirit; in Biblical creation the wind/spirit of God hovers over the water). The numerous allusions to the Creation in one poem turn those allusions into a metaphorical vehicle that conveys the lyrical narrator's account of creating her poem.

> "And love bursts out onto the whiteness
>   of the page
> Becoming the womb of my poem
> Hiding objects on the grass
> In the tonality of a soul living in great stillness
> Trembling like God
> Joining the whisper of the night."

While the first stanza was replete with Biblical allusions, the second stanza addresses directly the creation of the poem. The main reference is to conception: "becoming in the womb of my poem."

However, when the lyrical narrator says, "And love bursts out onto the whiteness of the page," she clearly refers to the birth of her poem, which is associated with bursting love, which is associated with a womb. "Hiding objects on the grass" may also serve as a metaphor for the Creation in Genesis (Chapter 2) when "grass" ("*essev*") is created. In this vertex of creation, even God Himself is trembling.

This poem contains a cluster of Biblical allusions to creation which metaphorically reflect the creation of the poem, exposing the latent mechanism of *ars poetica*.

ARCHES

Jerusalem clings to me in New York
Passes by in an oxymoronic course
Filled with splendor
And a heritage
And Mysteries
Against the arches of the heaven's dome
And stars like torches of fire
Rolling around and around
Among combinations of words like tunes
And sparks of vision
And fragments of stones
Crowding at the Wall
Against the din of the wind
And wanderings of the night
Strengthens within me.

The poem opens with the lines:
"Jerusalem clings to me in New York
Passes by in an oxymoronic course
Filled with splendor
And a heritage
And mysteries
Against the arches of the heaven's dome.

The oxymoron at the beginning of the poem can be plausibly explained; it is, indeed, an oxymoron to be in New York City while yearning for Jerusalem. As Yehuda Halevi, the renowned Hebrew poet who lived in Spain in the 11th century, put it: "My heart is in the East /And I am at the edge of the West."

The lyrical narrator of this poem laments her remoteness from Jerusalem, while being "exiled" in New York. Jerusalem is filled with inspiring splendor, imbued with rich heritage and beguiling mysteries; it is facing the arches of the dome of heaven.

Such an enchanting portrayal of Jerusalem seems to eclipse the powerful impression of New York. In fact, New York is mentioned only in the first line of the poem, as a place of exile, whereas the rest of the poem is dedicated to Jerusalem. The reference to New York acts as a trigger: once it is invoked, Jerusalem takes center stage, while New York is forsaken, marginalized.

"And the stars like torches of fire
Rolling around and around
Among combinations of words like tunes
And sparks of vision..."

This part of the poem, which is the most prominent, is cleverly constructed around an allusion to the vision of a sublime chariot in the book of Ezekiel:

"...a tempestuous wind blew from the north, an enormous cloud and flashing fire, surrounded by radiance...and the sight of the animals is like blazing coals and torches of scorching fire...and the animals are rushing all around .....when the animals moved forward, the wheels of the chariot moved at their side....and the tempestuous wind blew to the sides of the wheels...and the blowing wind was the wheels ....." (Ezekiel, chapter 1).

Thus, "the sparks of vision" in the poem clearly correspond to Ezekiel's sparks of vision, to his the

prophetic revelation, which is delivered like torching fire. Portraying Jerusalem as a prophetic vision, endowing it with glory and majesty, almost turns it into a heavenly city.

The subsequent description of Jerusalem focuses on its stones, on the Wailing Wall. However, it is also crowned with the splendor of holiness:

> "...And fragments of stones
> Crowding at the Wall
> Against the din of the wind..."

The poem concludes with:

> "...And wandering of the night
> And an almost specific sunrise
> Reinforces within me."

The wanderings of the night are followed by sunrise and this bestows on the poem some continuity and a unifying structure.

The fact that the sunrise is almost a specific one enables the reader to identify with the holiness and sublimeness of Jerusalem from an earthly, human perspective. The "almost specific sunrise" enables the poet to admire Jerusalem on both levels: the prophetic holiness and the earthly splendor (the sunrise is almost a specific one, not a heavenly one, as described earlier in the poem) and it reveals intimate closeness.

Thus, while Dickens wrote a tale of two cities, this poem tells a tale of two cities that turns into a tale of one city.

I EMBODY THE POEM

My splintered love yearns for the night
Inspires sorrow
On small paper benches

My death no longer matters.

I embody the poem
Feel it not just in my head
But it my mouth too:
Words have such power.

The poem focuses on the love of the lyrical narrator, as well as on the art of creating poetry. As stated earlier, the theme of creating a poem is one of the recurrent themes in the poetry of Edith Covensky.

The first stanza reads:

"My splintered love yearns for the night
Inspires sorrow
On small paper benches."

The paper benches bring to mind the art of writing poetry, since a poem—like any kind of literature—exists on paper. The splintered love, which yearns for the night, inspires sorrow. The stanza has a melancholic touch reminiscent of Anton Chekhov's plays, such as *The Seagull, Three Sisters, The Cherry Orchard,* and *Uncle Vanya.* The atmosphere in these plays is not one of crushing gloom and doom, but rather of lingering melancholy and serene sadness, profound unhappiness, frustration and autumnal blues. In *Three Sisters,*" the eponymous characters yearn to leave their dull, rural surroundings and settle in cosmopolitan Moscow. Yet they will never realize their dream. That sad recognition dominates the atmosphere of the play.

The same atmosphere permeates the first stanza of this poem. The love of the lyrical narrator is fragile; it inspires sadness and seems doomed to be short-lived.

As previously stated, the "small paper benches" remind us of the process of writing poetry since poetry is, for the most part, dependent on paper.

In the next part of the poem, the lyrical narrator states that her "death no longer matters." Such a statement transforms the initial sad atmosphere into a much more somber, mournful atmosphere with tragic, morbid overtones. The concluding stanza of the poem states:

"I embody the poem
Feel it not just in my head
But in my mouth too:
Words have such power."

The lyrical narrator turns into the poem itself. Thus she identifies to the fullest with her art. By being a poet, she communicates with her sorrowful love, and even with the tragic, haunting thought of death. Hence, her poem can reach out to the source of sadness, since "words have such power." Indeed, words have incredible power; with words a war is declared, with words a peace treaty is signed; with words the entire human civilization had been created. And with words poems are written.

SUMMARY OF A POEM

My verses are enveloped in silence
Flowing among my illusions
Restless
Seeking a title for me
A summarizing poem
By all accounts.

And in a scattered instant
Love comes to me
Rocking in its cradle
Rolling on the grass.

My soft words are befogged

Anxiety is here
Focused freely in the poem
Concealed in confusion.

Like many other poems by Edith Covensky, this poem, too, deals with *ars poetica*, with the art of writing poetry.

The poem opens with the statement:

"My verses are enveloped in silence
Flowing among my illusions
Restless
Seeking a title for me
A summarizing poem
By all accounts."

The first line is an oxymoron. Verses, which by their very nature "speak out," express in sound the poet's thought, are here "enveloped in silence." The themes, images and metaphors that produce the poem, are here frustrated, denied, muted.

And yet, the verses of the poem of the lyrical narrator continue, "flowing among my illusions/ restless." The illusions experienced by the lyrical narrator may relate to thwarted expectations.

The verses of the lyrical narrator are "restless" when they encounter the following paradox: the customary creative process whereby a poem is written by an "implied author" is here frustrated; the poem is the one that dictates to the "implied author" how to compose the poem. This may explain the "illusions" in the previous line.

This poem argues that the "implied author"—via his rhetorical vehicle, the lyrical narrator—is mistaken when he purports to be the one who determines the process of composition. According to this poem, such an expectation is only an illusion. The poem is not the "artistic tool" of the lyrical narrator (who, rhetorically, represents the "implied author"); the poem is the one that creates for the lyrical narrator its own "artistic tool," the one that writes the poem in accordance with the dictates and instructions of the poem itself.

Following that unexpected, dramatic reversal, the poem is also the one that dictates to the lyrical narrator what title to give the poem. Thus, it is the poem that composes the poem, and the lyrical narrator is nothing but a go-between who delivers information from the poem to the poem.

The right title for the poem—according to the directive of the poem itself—yields "a summarizing poem, /By all accounts." Thus, the poem conveys the idea that it is not the traditional poet who is the master of his/her poem, but rather the new concept: the 'summarized poem' is the one that summarizes itself.

"And in a scattered instant
Loves come to me
Rocking in its cradle
Rolling on the grass."

Although the second stanza of the poem focuses on love and not on the art of creating poetry, there is an obvious analogy between this stanza and the previous one. In both stanzas expectations are frustrated and common knowledge is challenged, proven to be wrong, and is replaced by a new knowledge. In the first stanza, the frustrated expectations occur when the reader is taken by surprise and notified that it is not the poem's "implied author" who creates the poem but rather the poem itself creates the poem. In the second stanza, we are told that the love that comes to the lyrical narrator is expected to be a mature, ripe love. But the second stanza denies such an expectation by declaring that the love is not mature but rather childish.

Love is portrayed as an infant ("rocking in its cradle") or as a toddler frolicking in the grass ("rolling on the grass"). One may argue that this paradox, this denial of natural, logical expectations, is already foreshadowed in the first line of the second stanza. "And in a scattered instant/ Love comes to me." Love, it would seem, has caught the lyrical narrator unprepared, just as the reader is unprepared when he/she

Arie Menes, Composition #02261408 ©

is notified that his/her natural, logical belief is completely wrong and should be replaced by another,
newly constructed belief (that a poem composes
itself).

"My soft words are befogged:
Anxiety is here
Focused freely in the poem
Concealed in confusion."

It is only natural that such frustrated expectations, ones that contradict human logic, will cause "soft, befogged words," and generate in the poet feelings of anxiety and confusion, which are concealed.

This *ars poetica* poem is extreme in the way it defies logical and conventional expectations. However, one can also frustrate the frustrating poem, the one that believes that it writes itself: it can only reach the reader through the consciousness of the lyrical narrator. The "victorious" party in this poem is not the poem that writes itself but rather the artistic skillfulness of the lyrical narrator (who rhetorically represents the "implied author") who writes the poem and delivers it to the reader.

LUCID SPEECH

I found my lucid speech
As antithesis to the lonely words
I heard in the street
That I might have written in darkness
In great haste.

But who would recall the exactness of words
Of the fluctuations of light

As they were entreated to rest on the page.

At most they would say
I had written another
The poetic record
Peeling its color dark
For the sake of love.

The entire poem deals with the most prevailing theme in Edith Covensky's poetry, *ars poetica,* the process of composing poetry.

The first stanza states:

"I found my lucid speech
As antithesis to the lonely words
I heard in the street
That I might have written in darkness
In great haste."

The lyrical narrator draws a distinction between lucid words (speech) which is the language of her poetry, and the words she has heard in the street, "vulgar" words, almost "sinful" words that the poet writes in darkness, in great haste, trying to hide her artistic "sinfulness" and "vulgarity." It seems that although the lyrical narrator is devoted to the lucid words of her poetry, she feels attracted to the "vulgar, "sinful" words she has heard in the streets. Those words of the street may have been written by the lyrical narra-

tor in darkness, in great haste, in order to conceal her "artistic iniquity." The lucid, "enlightened" words of poetry versus the "vulgar," "sinful", almost "profane" words of darkness, of the street, establish a contrasting analogy between the traditional, lucid words of poetry and the dark words of the street. It seems that the "vulgar, "sinful," obscure words of the street attract and fascinate the lyrical narrator; they have the allure of forbidden fruit. The words of the street are written in darkness, in great haste, since they are forbidden words, they are illicit, sinful words, traditionally considered inappropriate for writing poetry. Yet those attributes of the words of the street attract the lyrical narrator who is used to lucid words, the conventional material of poetry.

"But who would recall the exactness of the words
Or the fluctuations of light
As they are entreated to rest on the page."

The "vulgar", "sinful" street words may be considered "perilous" since they threaten the existence of the traditional, respectable, "lucid" poetic, words. Thus, once the lyrical narrator has tasted the forbidden fruit, the "illegal, "vulgar, "sinful" words of the street, her lucid words, the traditional, "legitimate" words of poetry will be forgotten, forsaken.

Such is the power of darkness that it threatens to invade the lucid, enlightened realm of poetry and banish the traditional, lucid words of poetry.

"At most they would say
I had written another
Thin poetic record
Peeling its dark color
For the sake of love."

Had the lyrical narrator been so strongly attracted to the "vulgar," "illegitimate," "sinful" street words, which traditionally are not permitted into the realm of the legitimate lucid words of poetry, she would have lost the appreciation of the traditional target audience of her poetry. Had she given in to the "sinful," "vulgar" words, her target audience would have turned against her. They may consider her poetry just "another thin poetic record," poetry that is devoid of substance and should therefore be eliminated.

And yet the lyrical narrator seems determined to pay a high price for abandoning the traditional lucid words of poetry. She is ready to become a pioneer in her use of those "vulgar," "illegitimate," "sinful" street words, instead of being in thrall to the traditional "lucid words" of poetry. She is willing to lose her traditional target audience, committed as it is to traditional, "legitimate" words of poetry, in order to follow her heart, her poetic credo.

Composing poetry with the newly adopted "vulgar" words of darkness is compared to "peeling the dark color" of the "thin poetic record;" her new, rebellious, unbridled poetry is considered "dark," since it has abandoned the traditional "worthy" words of poetry.

The final verse of the poem introduces two new words, which cast a new, surprising light on the entire poem. These words [two in the Hebrew original] are "for the sake of love." These two words invest the poem with a new meaning: the poem that records the attraction of the lyrical narrator to street "vulgar" "sinful" words of poetry, does not do it for the sake of poetry per se, but rather for the sake of love. The poem that up to now focused on the rebellious attitude of the lyrical narrator towards poetry turns out to be a poem about love. Whatever the lyrical narrator does, or does not do, it is not for the artistic purpose of composing innovative poetry, but rather for the sake of love.

Thus, the last two words (two in the Hebrew original) cast a new, surprising light on the poem as a whole, one that turns the entire poem on its head. The true motivation for abandoning the formal,

distinguished poetic words and adopting the vulgar prosaic words of the street is, in fact, a down-to-earth, emotional one: not for the sake of aesthetics but rather for the sake of love.

Thus the conclusion of the poem invests it with a whole new dramatic meaning. It exemplifies the most distinctive feature of literature: the dynamics of earlier and later information along the continuum of the text, whereby new information casts light on earlier one and alters the reader's perception of it.

I BECAME A MODERN PAINTER

I turn the day into fiction
Between, the clippings of the poem
In which may easily be read such things
As light shadow and the sea.

I became a modern painter
Crossing the borders of time
With summer emotions

And with amusing warmth
And almost waking rain.

Like numerous poems by Edith Covensky, this poem is also dedicated to *ars poetica*, to the process of writing poetry. However, every time a poem is associated with composing poetry, the point of view of the lyrical narrator changes, her way of observing reality changes, and the way in which the poem's fictional world conducts a dialogue with concrete reality changes as well. Hence, in every *ars poetica* poem, where the poem examines the relation between poetic fiction and concrete reality, the perspective of the lyrical narrator changes.

The first line proclaims the main creative function of the poet:

"I turn the day into fiction
Between the clippings of the poem
In which may easily be read such things
As light, shadow and sea."

The poem's source of materials is indeed mundane, everyday, routine; gray dull days turning into fiction, which is the poem, which is art, that which transcends humdrum reality. The text in this early part of the poem contains a paradox. Only when the dull day turns into fiction, once the everyday reality transforms into art—which is a poem—does the process of tracing elements in the artistic text—such as light, shadow and the sea—become easy, an effortless process.

Normally, things in reality and in fiction are opposites. Here is the challenging paradox, however. It is difficult to decipher art, poetry, while it is rather easy to comprehend and decode daily objects such as light, shadow and sea. In this poem, however, only when daily, humdrum reality turns into elevated art such as poetry, does it become easy to comprehend and interpret its symbolic meanings.

The second stanza in the poem reads:

"I became a modern painter
Crossing the borders of time
With summer emotions..."

There is an integrating link that connects this stanza to the first. In the first stanza lies a paradox: lofty art such as painting and poetry becomes accessible only when it turns into dull, routine, gray reality. It is lofty fiction that blazes a trail toward comprehending daily, routine, dull reality.

In the second stanza, the modern painter (the lyrical narrator) does not copy reality but rather invents an imaginary reality, as is the case in abstract, cubist, symbolist, expressionist, impressionist, Surrealistic and other schools of painting. Unlike the first stanza, where gray, dull reality can be interpreted only when it turns into lofty, challenging art (poetry in this case), in the second stanza the artist does not rely on daily reality but invents his/her own lofty, imaginary reality (such as in Symbolist poetry, for instance, or in Stream of Consciousness, in prose fiction ("lyrical novel", "psychological novel").

Paradoxically, the two stanzas of the poem are connected through a chiasm: the relations between poetry and reality in the first stanza are the opposite of the relations between the artist and reality in the second stanza. In the first stanza, poetry, art, is the tool that can help us decode dull, everyday reality. In the second stanza, the daily reality is dismissed and is replaced by artistic, lofty, symbolic reality.

In the second stanza, the lyrical narrator, the painter, crosses "the borders of time." As in the previous case of the painter, who dismisses daily reality in favor of imaginary reality, the painter who crosses the borders of time, also "sacrifices" the rules of everyday reality (limits of human time) in order to reach an unrealistic, limitless, timeless order of living.

The "summer emotions" that conclude the second stanza can be better comprehended when read in the Hebrew original. "Summer" in Hebrew is *"kai'tz,"* which etymologically derives from the noun *"ketz,"* meaning end, termination, conclusion. Hence, according to the original Hebrew, the modern painter does not only cross the borders of time, she also challenges the borders of summer, the borders of termination, of ending.

The third stanza concludes with:

"And with amusing warmth
And almost waking rain.

The lyrical narrator (the poet, the painter) continues crossing borders: she crosses the borders of time, she crosses the borders of emotions ('sensitivities' in Hebrew) of summer; she crosses the borders of the "amusing warmth;" she crosses the borders of the rain which is about to wake up (in the hot climate, the rain in fall and winter heralds awakening and growth; it is the period in nature when flora are budding and blossoming). The heat mentioned in the poem ("amusing warmth") is amusing, associated with pleasantness, since it is known that eventually fall and winter will take over and the scalding, scorching heat of summer will no longer be oppressive.

In such a short poem, the lyrical narrator dons three different masks: she is a poet, she is a painter, and she is also a wanderer who keeps crossing borders. And behind each mask, there is always the lyrical narrator who observes both art/poetry and reality in an insightful, discriminating, and inspiring fashion.

POETIC CANOPY: ANTHOLOGY OF SELECTED POEMS BY EDITH COVENSKY

All hundred and fifty Psalms
Cry out at once
(Yehuda Amichai)

A DELUSION

My love sparkles moving with the chirps of
summer
Like a bird with poured out longing
Flies enveloped in a game
Rolling in song
Merging with the trill of the night
Wanders among crooked alleyways
From fear of the shadows.

And I am an expert poet
Colliding in darkness
Striking my hammer
Shattering the ordinary
Splitting light from the dark
Turning in an arbitrary day
Deluding.

BALLAD

My eyes sparkle on you
Peeping as if coupled to the wind
Folded among envisioned flowers
Swaying in the landscape.

An oriental bird lives in me
Like the heroine of a ballad
Hearing God
Bursting through barriers with astounding talent
Sliding on the earth
Commemorating my poem.

How would you feel in my place
My poem is of an extreme type
Fleeting recognition
Hugging the night.

I INVENT THE SUN

I am caught up in the signs of day
Enchanted seduced in the flow
Between objects and symbols
Smudging the rules of the poem.

I hoard the breadth of the words
Invent the sun
As if grasping the celestial bodies
Hovering above all this.

Ever since I pierce my sadness across an
          archetypical sea
Gnawing away in the sand
Construct my poems daily
To conquer the dark.

POETIC INNOVATION

I am fiction
Bound up in the mystery of the words
Preserved in the text
Eagerly adopting my innovations
Amongst ordinary things
Memorable in winter.

I wonder
Making real the extent of my love
        with oft-used words
Circling around me like stars
Half laughing
Half crying
Playing a tune in a magical book.

My drawings are true
Because of my very longing for the sun
Made of yearned-for love
And an optimistic warm body
And cold sweat.

AN IDEA OF LOVE

My dream is alive
Revealing my desire
In accumulated writings
Like in the writing of a diary.

I become realized in illusion
An idea of a great love
Curling in silence
Mixed-up in a captive language.

What is all this noise
Rolling in the middle of the poem
Flowing between cuts of such a reality.

Without a poem I have no future
As though this connection lifts me
        through the ranks
Daring in love.

AN AVANT GARDE POEM

I roll one controversy to another
Combining an avant-garde poem
And a newly remembered hint
Realizing the night.

And I am at peace with this illusion
Playing between vision and reality
Sinking into me on such a day.

And I still evade the course of time
Astounded in a blue drawing
And in concealed irony
Moving me to the edge of speech.

OPEN LOVE

Your eyes are poetic
Assembling in me dizzily
Preserving the instant
Revealed on a scrap of my page.

My day drips water against revolving stars
Like open love
Strengthening in words
Flying like a bird mobilized to sing.

But that is just weakness at the time of writing
In the shadow of warm words
That even the night cannot cancel.

CONFESSION

My love accumulates from book to book
A portion so wondrous
A mixture complicated in words.

And my distress becomes a blessing
Among revolving stars
Branching within this maze.

I am drunk on love
Deviating from my dense time in a
great confession
And an instant of impulsive weakness
becoming beauty.

What day is set into a poem
The sum seems to be renewed
with much redness
Confusing me amidst musings
that become sketches
Amusements of imagination
Glorious in illusion.

WATERCOLOR (1)

I am complexly autistic
Between the tumult of time
And a memory of the night
Folded in the canvas
In some romantic yearning
Sketching my dream.

And the day is like a flower of love
Rolling in blue paint
In a watercolor
And things that assemble in a poem
Playing at love in me sweetly
In yellow lines seized in the sun.

YOU ARE SENSUAL

You are sensual
Bursting forth exactly in the poem
Among memories of things
Scattered in depth
Evaporating in fear.

My thought develops
Flourishes among rolls of my page
In testimony set into the night
Making my time.

I remain in confusion
Magnify your love in the sun
In the sparkle of a scrap of light.

WORDS IN BLUE

I pretend rhymes in refined pain
And desire captive in my memory
Bursts my supposing joyfully
Teasing my lips.

My love joins the suggestions of the poem
Heaven descends to the earth
Drenched in sun
Portrayed from the apex of the day.

And then I slip out of fear
Dense in light and noise and mountain
Portraying words in blue
Flowing in a poem like this.

Arie Menes, Composition #05041309 ©

FOR GABRIEL PREIL (1)

Preil bedecks himself on a New York street
As if focused on creation
Drawing with autumnal tongue
A clear chronology
Fluid in my imagination
Touching eternity.

What bluish romanticism infiltrates through me
Heavenly evading in the night
Caught in my quick eyes
In a future yellow page.

And the words revolve within each other
In my great synthesis
Dropping on confused pages
In a monologue becoming a poem.

FOR BRUNO

I create my poem in a chronology
From a balcony overlooking the sea
Freely using music
As in the rustle of the night
Enthusiastically satirical.

And the vista flies in the summer
      like a blue airplane
Always departing on time.

I have room to think about the night
And about the words that surround me
Especially now
Without limit
As a linear playfulness.

And then I clothe my memories
      with accurate sun
Playing in this field
With illusions crossing time.

I WRITE IN CONFUSION

I write in confusion
Between laughs
Tired with mirth mixed in the night
Wondering rolling things
Bursting from twilight to twilight.

And you infiltrate crowded between the columns
Absorbing my voice
Bundled in great darkness
Tense on my notebook of poems.

What love scorched on my flesh
Pierces me with new illusion
Illuminating some truth for me.

SUMMERS

My love serves as challenge for me
Dizzying me in the poem
Awakens longing in me
In a hot tumultuous day
Revolving in the landscape of a summer like this.

My eyes spin
In an unbridgeable distance
Sinking in a table of ancient times.

As I sit wondering amidst the ruins
Like an anti-hero
Strolling in water soaked words.

It is already hard for me to say
anything in loneliness.

PSYCHOSIS

My thought is wild
Erupting from the quiet
In a city of gardens
And in verses opening the poem.

I erase time
In the sinking of night begetting stars
As if returning the light to me.

My dream curls in longing
Passes with a low hurry like grass
In a psychosis floating in new sadness.

Here the earth is closer to heaven like a bird.

I INVENT MYSELF EYES

I am no prankster
Constructing my poem
In compressed speech
Close to a new time
That perfumes my words
Amidst the swirling of the wild.

And I am a free woman
Rushing to the sea
On an axis of fluid time
Inventing myself eyes
And a language of stars
Moving the night.

ODE

My love is borne in memory
Established in this withdrawal
Bedecked in a gaiety of summer
Addicted pure to the sun.

And my excitement is marvelous
In converging story
Caught like chance harmony in a tune
Uniting in such a drawing of desire.

And then I walk to the edge of the night
Elegantly mingle with the poem
Touching things in a symmetry of day
Broken in the sea.

TO THE SUN

My mother hovers over me
Flowing like star against star
Curling immaculately among the words.

And she plays routinely
Desiring sun
Compressed in my memory
Sweeps me around and around
Striving to take flight in the wind.

There is a symbol here:
Open heaven covers me
Enfolded in quiet love
Circling with joy
Hurrying in the thin moment
Like God.

WINTER

My poem is a surviving yearning
Flowing in a chair of blue stars
Swaying at sunset
Burned with arousal.

My quiet is imaginary
Inventing marvelous things
Quoting philosophy
With sane humor
Evading me
Bursting from my memories.

And I adorn myself with a tune
Become excited in metaphorical language

Reveling in astonishment
Swept up in winter day
Laughing barrenly.

DISPUTATION

I dispute in the night
In a kind of all-encompassing essay
Fastened to the landscape
Murmuring words in silence

I have my own reality.

And God hovers here like an illusion
Gathers my love
Enters it into the day's agenda
In a snatched version
Bursting eccentrically
Turning over in my head.

What is all this sensitivity
Decoded touching me
Subject to time
Rolling within me
Garnered as for a beautiful woman.

PENCIL DRAWING

My day is swept away in a quiet revolution
Bursts in memory among musical drawings
Scurrying near me
To the edge of things.

I play in loneliness
Evade the night
With a pencil draw a few signs
Like earth
And a tree
And a flower.

And further I apologize for the errors in language
And for late musings
And too-simple words
Confused on a yellow page.

TEMPTATIONS

I write confession after confession
Revealing temptations stubbornly
Laughing in a wet day
Among shadows clear in the landscape.

I become popular
Sing like a night bird
Crowded lively in illusion
Living as through bestowing beauty on things.

I do not deny my deceptions
Touch the slate of memory
With a reflection like a poem
Between words yellowing in the sun.

I AM AN ANARCHIST

I am an anarchist
Drawing a fantasy of the sea
In a language I create on sand.

You amuse me
Only you exist in illusion
Turning in such silence
Set into the gallery of the poem
Celebrating my story.

What is this whole revolution
Churning in gaiety
Gathering in a monograph of night.

THE FLOWERS ARE PLUCKED
FROM EACH OTHER

I construct a poem
In a dialogue occurring beyond words
Clowning rashly near the source of light
Riotous in symbiosis

My day revolves sparkles among shades.

And you coddle yourself with humor
Amusing among the stars of light
Yearning for playful joining
Subject to time.

The flowers are plucked from each other
Scattered among the packets of sonnets
Preserved golden in my rhymes.

AN OPEN VISTA

My love lives
The pearl of day suits my dream
Concentrated in a night biography
Authentic according to all signs.

And I am addicted to the poem
Based upon pondering
Bedazed in an open vista
Facing stars echoing in invention.

This is something much more spiritual
Renewed among the other legends.

NIGHT FALLS ON NARROW STREETS

Night falls on narrow streets
And the moon crumbles the day
And intensifies gloom

And preserves the contrast
Between day and night
Preserves time.

I save from all these
A trampled leaf falling
On the pages of the book

And trampled dry flower
And the thin wing of a butterfly
And a wing of a plane.

IMPRESSION

My day's current rises
Soaked in earth-colors
And my laughter wits

My face is chaste
My utterance simple at sunset.

And from the stream of my
       autobiographical poem
Made impure as if useless
Rises my experimental voice

Like the voice of a water bird.

We are two people who love
       (you say)
Not revolutionaries
Fragile products
At low sun.

MONOGRAPH

I found a hint of joy in you
And positive energies
And even dedicated to you
A monograph of love.

You hesitated for a while
Stayed in the kingdom of your poems
Influencing in the night
The next verse.

The order of words was not accidental
My diary was clinical
With no signs of childishness

And you did not notice the woman in love :
The operator at play.

BLESSINGS

As on wine my blessing is on love
Believing with ease that beauty saves
And that the sun is like a window
Above the heights of the eyes.

I have traded smiles with a boy in the street
Indicating playfully
A birth certificate
An identity card
In a chronicle of nowhere else.

My body was frozen in dance
Yours has beguiled me to forget
Whirled me into its own reality
Approaching the close.

SIGNS OF TIME

I contemplated your confusion
My eyes searched your depths
With burning letters on the edge of language.

I was silent
Because of the night's weight
Thought after thought
And soft weaknesses
And afterwards the color
Of thin rain.

I saw stars
And the sun suspended on its axis
As symbols of time
The living drew me.

My basic fear stays with me as
        long as the sand.

ODESSEUS

A lover's wind plays and schemes in me
Exchanging signs of secrecy
Among the cats on a tense street.

The shape of man shocks me
Hung like a cloud
Dusty from the attempts
Begun in my wanderings.

My spirit springs up like a storm
Touching me and not touching
Fastening my lips to the night
In such aloneness.

EXPECTED LOVE

A woman is writing a poem : creating illusions
Without exact definitions
And of no school.

Love exists in her head
And still more in her momentary silence
Playfully.

The rain's chemicals no longer frighten her
Her smile is legible on her forehead
Her tongue does not fail

And what she writes lives only
        in the page's center.

METAMORPHOSIS

At the loveliest instant
I am silence or laugh
Pass color between the words
In handwriting crowded and quiet.

And my time is lost
Like the last page of a novella
Passing quickly over a flat page
And mingles in me to be bird
Or flower.

Sun and tree and sand fall together
Just when I write.

A POSSIBILTY FOR POETRY

I feel more elevation of spirit
Charmed by the possibility of poetry
In the dim high night
Try to seize time
And the tempo of your breath.

From my point of view
This is a day's attempt
An embodiment of your being
The first breakthrough
Appeasing even God.

I BECAME A DEBAUCHED PHILOSOPHER

The shadow of the night
Dresses in dismal beauty
And my charming sadness
And drunken laughter
Awaken love in me.

My illusion is dreamlike
Like memories of my excitement.

I became a debauched philosopher
Amidst the waves of perfume

And the deceptions
And my spirit a wandering exile
And my limits: the sea.

MY MOTHER PERCEIVED AS FICTION

My mother perceived as fiction
Her walk fetching
Her body composed of my pranks

And she is energetic and daring
Her windings staying beyond reality.

Her place is sublime
The wrinkles on her face separate and combine
Her dress is blue
Her motion: a flower
Enclosing all summers.

TRACES OF LOVE

Traces of love are suspended
Each with its own language
Appearing to me in a dream

And easy wonder plays on my face
Frolics freely on the screen of my worlds.

My attempt at love is stubborn
Ethereal in amazement
Yoked to the coach of my soul
Playful on the page.

At moments my existence transpires faultlessly.

SUNBEAMS

My poem is made like grid
Absorbing your possible love
And the light it emits
At this hour.

My eyes stare in darkness
Whispering among the stars
Lyrical on my own terms

And the poem reveals your face
Radiant reviving your memory
Celebrating in my invention.

I ALSO HAVE THE TEMPER OF POETS

I also have the temper of poets
The burden of my legacy in its realistic measure
Arouses some important love.

And perhaps I have no true rendition
        of this poem
My love is plaited in my mouth
Twined in my breast
On ordinary days.

As far as I am concerned
This is a dated biography
Crumbs of thoughts
A song anticipated
Justifying its own existence.

MY DAY BEGINS WITH WATER

My day begins with water
And the salt remains in the mouth
And the sun bends time
On the dead landscape.

There is beauty in this world
And there are flowers in the wind
And there is also sun
As Vivaldi writes in his music
"The Seasons."

Telegraph wires connect now to every pole
And they slice through the air
And they are tall.

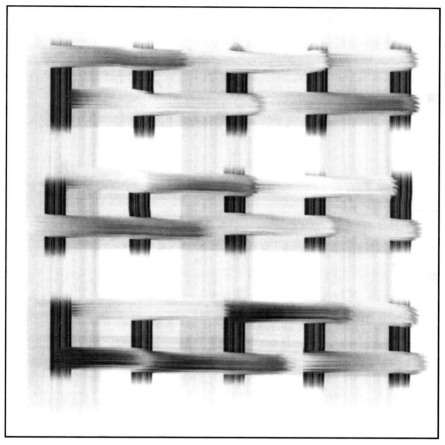

Arie Menes, Composition #05011313 ©

ANALYSIS

A few times I thought to myself :
No sign will remain of my life
Or any sign of heaven
On earth
And then I will be buried in the sea
Like a fish

And then grass will sprout from me
And blood will rise in the grass
And water will arise in the blood.

A war leaves signs
And a plane crossing the sky
Leave signs

Like a bird.

POETICS

The mysticism of the soul
Is sometimes a revelation of my lucidity.

My work is an abstraction
Of landscapes
And thoughts.

Ashbery repeats the formula of Horace:
Poetry is like painting.

It is easy for me to write
Easy for them to draw.

When I write now
I permit myself
The greatest freedom.

FOR MAGRITTE

1929
Words are constructed as signs
Language within language
(Said René Magritte).

Words have significance :
A black cat is not a cat
A red flower is born from the earth

A leaf can be a cannon
A cloud may be sun
Sun can be a cloud.

Words alone bind me to the tree.

SYNTHESIS

My poem mingles with a droplet of your tear
Exposes analogical sensitivities
Stamped in me since my birth.

I free myself from conventions
Touch the edges of the green
And above me are countless stars.

My thought has been defeated
You have burst into
The chambers of my mind
And my mute desire is tempted
In the flood of impressions and memories
Effortless.

Arie Menes, Composition #02261411-1 ©

AN AVANT GARDE PAINTING

I am swept up in the poem
Spiral among red flowers
As in a great space
Of an avant garde painting.

My dry eyes are filled with time lost to me
In a cumulative current within me
My poem: a sea.

And you hover between the forms of my lips
Your love flickers mysteriously
Wandering with new hope.

And then the water is reflected
*   on the rim of my day*
In yellowing light
Pretending to be sun.

A FLOWER OF DRUNKENESS

I delude myself
Clear-headed calm between
fragments of my verse
Mocking out of excitement
At a moment of chanted love.

I have such desire
Emerging between the words
Crowded in silence.

And the poem is born
A sublime halo entangled within me
Enfolded in pure writing.

And something primal rises from the water
A flower of drunkenness
A kindled ode runs in me
Tumbles on the page.

TO PLATO

Your love astounds
Open to the night
A kind of declared musing on a rational page
Flooding the landscape.

And my speech is naked to the edge of confusion
Analytical at the tip of the paintbrush
Tempting between the lines
Revolving in Platonic awkwardness
Uplifting my soul.

What love courses through me
In speech frugal
Its edge slippery
Bound in the poem.

THE SILENCE INSULATES ME

I acquire your love
A live flower warming in the sun
Fragile between dream and dream
Diluted among syllables of the night.

Here starts the clarification
Adorning itself
Exposed to the poem
Looking at me with sad eyes
A faint smile on my lips.

And the memory is within my reach
Your shadow curls on the wall
Revolves in creation signifies

The silence insulates me.

FIRST RAIN

My lips are silent among the delusions
A kind of a geological layer placed on the page
Undated
Carefully folded.

And the landscape is dark where the road bends
And a first rain rustles between the words.

Signs of my day are exposed
Edges of my time are blurry
Silence erupts
Combines with the sea.

And the words are in my reach
Fragrances of night flowers
Wafting in amusement.

VOICES OF THE SEA

The poems rush to me
In words of shadow and memory
Squadrons in the night unfolding on the scene.

And a voice of the sea leaps in motion
Like a bird on a proper course
Flies to her origin
Journeying on the mountain of God.

Thus is the idea of the poem born in me :
A curled wick of God
An exact autumnal sign
Founded within me.

LOVE EMBRACES LOVE

Love embraces love
Flourishes at the touch
Thaws into life after coldness
Beautiful as the sea.

Quiet and virginal.

And after love has survived
The basic creation clings to me
In rhymes new and old
As in a thawed instant of song.

I AM ADDICTED TO ILLUSION

I am addicted to illusion
Annul time between the folds of water
My self-amused desire flows
My poem: a feather.

And my eyes are revealed in the clear redness
Defining the day as if I were a painter
My language realizes my love.

And the poem is a sketch like a flower
Living in precious light
Shaking free like a dancing winged bird
Is sun absorbing sun.

STILL LIFE

You feel my loneliness
As an allegory of my human existence
But this is not reason enough to freeze the day.

I speak from my dream
Hiding behind the obsession
Surrendering to your glance.

My small world is great
Also laden with stars
And completely open view
And a scent of colors in a silent painting.

IN THE BEGINNING

I collect stars
Like rolling words
In the kindness of night
And a memory of wind
And a musical room
And a laughing girly
Against the fray of things
In the rustle of a night and day
And around Jerusalem moon
And longings bound in a net of time as this.

What do I need all the holiness
And the visions
And the words cascading in the
*   signature of my hand*
In a chronicle of fall
And great darkness
And a full sea
And a bird separating water from water.

I BECAME A DREAMER OF JERUSALEM

I became a dreamer of Jerusalem
Crossing time
In colorful illusion
Plunging in my depths
Between chapters of a paradoxical day.

The rocking is human on these pages
Gripping the base of the wall
The freedom limiting my scope.

And my poem is a secret
My survival is a puzzle knotted
        with exaltation of soul
And shattered longings.

SERAPHIM

I blaze a trail for a poem
In Jerusalem loneliness
Against open music
Living with me
Full of sun
And mighty waters
And lightening
And thunder
And eye to eye
Like Adam and Eve
Touching me in a cacophony of words
And wind
And God walking in the rustle
At a pure height
Flying in time revolving in summer
Like a black sea
And a girl's pain creates all the Seraphim.

YOUR DAWN JERUSALEM

Your dawn Jerusalem is pure white
      and innocent
Your wall a mighty light
Filling my existence.

Your forehead is childlike
Your love bursts forth in short verses
In the courtyard of my house.

Daughter of time
Exposed to the eye of the sun
Shining in darkness

Your rocks are shown reddening
Strewn between the words
Facing a wall
And helmets
And ceramic jars overturned on the floor.

I WAS CREATED IN THE IMAGE

I was created in the image
Engulfed in a street puddle
In the wind
In the rain
And in the secret of a tear
Among lines of a poem
And childhood wanders in a
        game of sun and sand
In a confession lifted up to heaven.

How many stars
How much shadow close to me
In matters of such darkness
And renovations of God
And soul spiraling like a bird above a wall
Bursting in memory
In the clamor of day
And wide time crowding on the scroll.

I SIT IN AN ICY LANDSCAPE

I sit in an icy landscape
Unwooded and torn
Raven and hard

And Jerusalem opens
Her powers before me
Concealed in a womb of her stones
Concealed in courses of stones
Like courses of words in lines
Words.

In the night I remove them
One by one
Two by two
And discover a great Byzantine stone
And Byzantine sand
And wood.

ETERNAL CITY

God creates Jerusalem
From yellowing stone
And chronological wood
Under a pure sun
Beginning the day.

And I combine words of light
In specific speech
Like a synopsis of a soul
And the whistle of wind
And a high street
Going from bank to bank.

And then I throw stars up to heaven
In an ancient night
Melting in the rhythm of a poem
And in the circle of time
And the mercy of splendor.

A POEM IN PROSE

My poem is a draft
Delicately charming to the point of pain
A stain of color on parched soil
A living plot among the ruins.

Great love arises from these words
Moving signs
Opening points of spring
Are hidden in them.

And my day is silent
Passing from word to word
Free in combination.

How I erupt blending in the poem
My wanderings long in the sunset.

TESTIMONY

My eyes quiver drunkenly
Bear my loneliness like a scarlet bird
Silent among the droplets of darkness.

My time is entwined in the poem
Like the testimony of the poet
And a silent promise
Spinning magic.

I am a woman of dreams:
My light is shadow
A fictitious sun embroiders my words
Scented in flight
Open to love.

WORDS BINDING WORDS

My puzzle poem is clarified in festivity
Drawn to the sun in concentrated intensity
Gusts in deception
Nobly mobilized in tune.

And I am like a shore bird
Gliding in this optimism
Grayish aware of the light
Shaking free in my flight.

And the words bind words
In an enthusiastic scheme revealing my song
Devised in me in summer.

Arie Menes, Composition #03021410 ©

CYCLICAL LOVE

My love is made from my cycle of poems
And from the recommended conciliation
And from the quotidian dreams.

And I adorn myself with a musical painting
Folded within me
Between the pairs of words
Playing peacefully almost like God.

I find nothing here except the sun
Tepid in bedecked optimistic tale
Enchanting in its confusion.

I even have young primitive bubbling words
Refined by light
Intimate on the first pages
In order to extract from me
In order to fly.

A KIND OF PAINTING

My mother enriches my day
Enthusiastic in this kind of painting
Sane in memory
Connects to the wind.

How many words I said to her
Signs revolving in a hiatus of new time
Concrete on this bench
Admiring the precision
In lack of time confused
Mingle with heat.

And everything because of the desire for sun
And because of my summer
Not that this is some story defined
Or just a list
Or another recommended poem.

I AM SILENT AS A FLOWER

My love hot in the midst of illusion
Lifts off in splendor among lucid memories
Washing over my window.

And children play among flowers
Entwined in loneliness
Blushing at sunset
Shaking themselves off at dawn.

I am silent as flower
Created in light engulfing me
Glowing in my path
Roaring with a smile
Falling silent.

MY WEAKNESSES ARE SCATTERED WITHIN ME

My freedom is funny
Turning in me with temptation
My weaknesses are scattered within me.

And I grasp in the vacuum
Stubbornly airy in debate
Flowing to create myself.

The formulation is clear
An exercise in moving thought
As I dependent on the sun.

And my game flourishes in the poem
My writing is fiction from flower to flower
Arousing my delusions.

The sophistry is strong :
One poem is lost and another preserved
Each time recreating my essence.

ORIENTAL LAMENTATION

My dream is drawn in free rhythm
Mixed with alchemy
Whirling among streets of sand
Clothed in sad beauty.

The music is desire and sadness
Floating like oriental lamentation
Among rare flowers.

What feeling appeases me
My laughter is drunken
My body wanders exiled

This is possible only thanks to the wind.

SONG BIRD

I draw words and symbols on the earth
Stamped in my language
Thin engulf me
Rolling in laughter and sobs.

I became a song bird
Rejoicing in my young voice
Quivering in the tumult with a clown's smile.

And love grows dizzying
Echoing within me
The impulse whispers within.

CONFESSION

My mother yearns for the sun
Ascends drenched in light
Perfumed in delusion.

Her puzzling being confuses with imagination
Connecting me to the poems.

She is my great deliverance
Exulting among the words
In sophisticated rhymes from pole to pole
Whispering in trance.

And I flow in this excitement
Whirl dazedly
Melted into the sunset
Poured out to the stars.

IN THE CRADLE OF POETRY

I depend on the pranks of time
My voice echoes with longing
My love invents your being.

My hand clasps your mysteries
Trembles with a new vision
My wintery day wanders
Rocking in the cradle of your song.

And the words shatter in nothingness
Flower from my throat at sunset
Crouch on my lips
Mingle with the wind.

I AM AN ANONYMOUS POET

I am an anonymous poet
Coming from the absurdity between
        light and darkness
Seeping into a fictitious poem
With a love rising from my dream.

And my day churns in me rustling
Flutters within me
In a disorder of voices
Magically holding me.

My joy is mischievous because of the toils.

And suddenly I have the urge to love
With transparent words
Stopping time
In a quick sentimental instant.

NOSTALGIA

I have strong nostalgia in my head
Laden with memories greater than I
For I see them now
Like heroes from history
In narrow striped clothing
As if from the war.

There is no place under the sun
Where you will not see such men
Sometimes as large as Goya's giant.

Perhaps in these stars they seem
Each man in his fashion
Late in this night.

AN APOCOLYPTIC WIND

I circle as fast as the wind
And my broad shadow hovers
Breaking forth against the curves of my body

Amidst the little light remaining.

And a tree grows on half of the world
An idiotic minimalist
Upsetting my balance.

And what is hard in me is left hanging
And the light is yellow like the crust of the earth.

Last words I heard were my vow of silence
In a scenery of sea
Rocking from star to star.

A YELLOW STAIN

My poem is preserved
Turning with the suppleness of day
In a stain of yellow light
Steep in the sun.

I have an obligation to the night
Like a black presence
Symbolic
Thought wholly a sinner.

From childhood I absorb all I see around me
In a strange landscape
And carnival air
Blowing in gaping darkness
And in the noise of high waters.

ANNE FRANK

I spin in an autobiographical poem
With the revolution of the night
And shadows move forward in order
Breaking on a tablet
Reminding me of all the graves
With perception open to the sky
Becoming dizzy at time of dark
And longings of a girl
Opposite silence
And a wasteland
And pure pain
Like a tear bursting out among the
        multitude of words
In red
And black.

I INVENT THE SUN

I am caught up in the signs of the day
Enchanted seduced in the flow
Between objects and symbols
Smudging the rules of the poem.

I hoard the breadth of words
Invent the sun
As if I am grasping the celestial bodies
Hovering above all this.

Ever since I pierce my sadness across an
Archetypical sea
Gnawing away in the sand
Construct my poems daily
To conquer the dark.

AN IDEA OF LOVE

My dream is alive
Revealing my desire
In accumulated writing
Like in the writing of a diary.

I become realized in illusion
An idea of great love
Curling in silence
Mixed-up in a captive language.

What is all this noise
Rolling in the middle of the poem
Flowing between cuts of such reality.

Without a poem I have no future
As though this connection lifts me
          through the ranks.

CLAUSTROPHOBIA

Night becomes for me a possible reality
Minimal in silence
Among slippery bellflowers
As if invited to dance.

And I break in the fractures
Manage to speak the words
Strain to deceive myself
Erasing my shadow in an open notebook
Among imaginary flowers
In an almost claustrophobic room.

AN AXIOM OF LOVE

I am appeased with a memory of love
Revolving in illusion
Like an experimental dream
Joining a formula of a day
Hurried
Circular

Caught in the renewal of time.

And my poem slips away from the remainder
        of the night
In a swift composition
Becoming between the words
Lifting itself opposite the sun
With a joy of the hour playing within me
In the logic of the poem.

QUICK SPEECH

I live in a fracture of time
And dim memory
And clamor of day
Enmeshed in the archive of the wind.

And the speech is quick
Like a sound flowing in a catalogue of night
Curling in the light
Against the highest stars.

And the poem is caged in my mind
Among things of love
Dictating the course of words
Rolling with a yellow pencil.

SIGN LANGUAGE

My mother curls in the poem
In the tumult of day
And in the thicket of lonely time
Coded between the words.

And the cycle of her blood is in my blood
Flowing in the end of time
In sign language next to the night
Whispering in the uproar of the wind.

And my speech is revealed in an
          attempt at a poem
And in the murmur of a tiny tear
Serving the rain.

EQUATIONS

I have the ability to adapt
In a document of a poem
And in the cycle of a page pursuing a page
In reciprocal time
Flowing like water
And fertile stars echoing
In verses perfected with clarity
        of the equation
Among things of God
Resembling music
Touching till heaven
Commingled in a round street
Caught in the tension of the wind
Played like a dirge
Erupting at a point of night.

PROMETHEUS

I am an artist of the night
Jotting down words at the sweep of sadness
And the power of delusion
Stealing fire
Between signs of a flowing day
In the order of a poem
In sanity
And in thin talk
Pure
Turning with the logic of compressed time
And a flower enfolding between all the words
In an instant of triumphant writing
*   like words of God*
And the kindness of rain.

PURE DELUSION

I am a laughing woman
Sliding in a geographical poem
Between words of love gathering in the day
In a book of memories
In a white moment
Stiff
Deceptive in place and in time
Breaking like pottery
In a drunken summer
Like lust curling in the wind
And lofty longing
Alive in the rhythm of a bird
Adorned with beauty
Taking off into useful space
Twisting in pure delusion.

I MOVE BY THE MOTION OF THE STARS

I move by the motion of the stars
With the speed of lucid time
And love growing from the earth
Collecting twilight
In the glare of the shade
With a blessing
And a curse
As if with the language of children
In the funniest version
And beauty of enchantment
And a tipsy dream
As if there were nothing else.

PLANETARIUM

My mother is conservative
Gliding at the opening of a condensed poem
Near the sun
Swarms with great light
In the quick motion of wind.

And she has time of her own
In the cycle of sunrise and sunset
Across things of God
And stars interlaced.

And she is pure in the lightness
        of a brilliant instant
As if inventing water
Hovering without blemish
Lifting herself to the highest peak.

PICTO-POESIE

My time is round
Airy
Blue
Across a folding sea
In a picture of a poem
Joined to rain
Among stars hidden like matter of God
And delusions sliding down to the sea
Breaking up against water
And rain in the sad street.

And I write with the speed of wind
In a place engendering love
And such logic
And trembling words
Free infiltrating in exaggerated thought
In an order of illusions
And memory flowing in the middle of the day.

Arie Menes, Composition #05031305 ©

ON THE BORDER OF WATER

The poem: radiance
Infinite
An entity rousing within me
Clear on the border of water
Dragged at the edge of the street
Wet
Moving between grasses
Alive in the force of the wind.

Time frightens me
Like people milling about between rebellious
shadows
In a white night
Breaking
Like childhood rising at the
        awakening of an instant.

And I grow old like Homer
Covered by water
And yellow sand
Under stars available for love
And the tide of a single tear.

THE POEM IS AN INVENTION OF GOD

The poem is an invention of God
Like a warm memory
And festive flowers
In a scroll of a day
Rolling like water
Flowing with the absurdity of pain
Drawn on the page
Across a plastic bird
Rocking in space
At a used moment
And quickest night.

How I breathe in the womb of the poem
Living like Borges
In a play of illusions
And a longing folds within me
Across a revolving sunset
At the flutter of time
And an open sea
Silent
Roaring from bank to bank.

A NEW YORK POEM

I gather myself into this poem
As in an archetypical biography
Revolving in simple words
Wondering in the flow.

My love is lucid
Revealed in a New York plot
Thrilling in an impulsive night
Composed of white stars.

And I perfume myself with expectation
Dream on a banal day
Stubborn in illusion
Whispering words in blue light
Dissonant.

I QUOTE BERGSON

I quote Bergson
In a scene of childhood
Excited from memory to memory
In links of words suited for me
Turning the moment to eternity.

Time works on me
Trickling within me in a great enigma
Like rapid wind encircling me
Flexible in fantasy
Bursting out with such clarity.

I do not protest
Finally I circle free
Steal love
Mischievous playing in the poem
Like a girl in water.

A PAINTING BY EDVARD MUNCH

Your love is drawn on my body
Like a quick biography
Gleaming in the sun.

Your existence continues in the poem
Rambling amid polished words
Tall trees
Are growing at my side.

I inherited a physical memory
Multi-layered
Amid chains of time
Dead-alive
Screaming like in Munch's painting.

I AM NOT A NIHILIST

I am not a nihilist
Occupied with the precision of words
Feeling music
Fragile in the night
Giving birth to a poem
At a juncture of paradoxical time
Compressing stars
Across a love engendering love
Blitzing in the flow
Turning around in memory
Compiling my dreamy matter
In an orderly drawing on the sand.

I DELUDE MYSELF

I devote myself to night
Clinging to murk
Exchanging silent words
Among bouquets of blue flowers.

My memory turns in time
Burgeons amid optimistic words
Summarized in the poem.

I delude myself
Festive amid the tricks of day
Compressed in play
Laughing in a summer scene
Drawing fictional words
Flowing in delusion.

A WATER DRAWING

My mother curls up in a new monograph
Focused in invention
Sketching my delusions in a torrent of the poem
Like a drawing overflowing water.

And she envelopes herself in rhymes
Addicted to a scheme of the night
Avant garde dreaming among stars
In a quick landscape turning to memory.

And the words gather
Puzzling on an enchanting day
Unfolded like symbols of God.

THE WORK OF AN ARTIST

Time works on me
Across blue clouds of memory
Existing within me
Containing love contesting the night.

And I am like a modern stockman
Freezing a moment of excitement
And molds of pure thought
And an artist's audit.

Then whatever I succeed in creating
        plays in me
Across wind
And rigid matter
And a sad code of a poem.

A MAELSTORM OF NIGHT

My love flows in the zone of night
Becoming an adventurous star
Roaming in the maelstrom.

And I wander in this monologue
Enthused like a hilarious poet
Turning symbols to words
Focusing on summer.

And my hand is open in the poem
Drawing a flower within a flower
My tear rolls across the beacon of the night
Like darkness refined in light.

MYTHOLOGY

My mother speaks at night
Circles among the folders of my notes
And her eyes are open gleaming
Rolling with longing.

And I am like a bird of the skies
Flying from window to window
Curling in the silk of the wind
Photographing noble stars
Gathering in my head.

My night is a myth
Revolutionary heavy with words
Rushed split in summer
Living in the slant of night.

A WEAVE OF WORDS

I am silent with the blessing of night
Across a tear of God
And a vision of smoke
In a version of sorrow
And things in rhymes
And a useful memory
With the advantage of the whisper.

And then I laugh among the remainders of stars
Across from a field bird
And the water narcissus
In a wave of words
A place reminiscent of yellow time
And a used stone realizes the poem.

I AM A MYSTIC

I am a mystic at a time that has no other
Tramping in the void of night
Rustling in a wintery landscape
Sneaking in longing
Stormy in the poem's version
Amused in me
Trapping with a caress
Pointing at an enchanted illusion
Howling a dream
Praised in this formulation
Playing with water.

OBSESSION

I flow in the landscape
Playing a sleepwalker
In obsessive prose which encircles me
Like a world view printed in trembling.

And my breath is light
Sprout rare primitive flowers
In a field of light
Curling in illusion.

And I go from existence to existence
Erasing the rain
Float across a large sea
As though rustling in a dream.

A NATIVE FLOWER

You play for me
Creating brilliant words
Violins of enchanted silence
Lucid in my memory
Trapped in the bundle of your love
Alive in thought
Giving birth to a native flower
Impressive in red.

A DREAM ARTIST

I am a dream artist
Wandering in the poem
In the whiteness of night
Tie my scatterings
With love resting within me
Whispering words flowing across from God
Longing for the splendor at such a moment
Sliding like a star on the sea.

MYSTICISM

I add stars to the night
Signs in the middle of the sky
Love in its own shadow
Hurries in the flow
Silent crowds into my head
Enthuses me with the sun's beauty
And hot earth revolves among all the words.

A SEA SQUALL

I erupt against the sea
And crowded waters flow with the haste of day
And with the intuition of wind
And color of the earth
And a thought harboring at a time
        revolving in the poem.

And my love is enchanted in the trial of night
And a veil of dream
And stars thriving in the heavens
Like careful rhymes on an open page
Decorated with clear language
Like a private joke
And soft yearning
And primary words
Turning in a blue summer.

FOR NOVALIS

My pain is akin to the night
Flowing in blue time
Roaming among shadows
Squared on the page.

And I bend a flower
With warm desire
Create a poem
And a sandpiper bursts through a
       riddle of such a day.

And the speech is revealed
Selective
Full of beauty
And clear music within me
Visible in this invention.

FOR PROMETHEUS

I have plenty of things near the poem
Indicating words according to the night
Living like Prometheus
Stealing fire
Trapping love in an instant dream
Singing with a flute tight against the wind
Enfolding between the lines
Crowded with pure language
Amid the stains of evil laughter
Hoarding time falling into water
In a landscape flowing to the formless dark
Rolling in dizzying drawing
Closing on a memory.

A BLUE BIRD

My illusion becomes
Cropped from the power of the night
Like a fancy drawing up stars.

And love cleaves to me
Glinting in the give of time
Touching me like a flower
And warm sand
And softest earth.

And the poem plays in a strange moment
Like a marginal pause
And the longing of a blue bird circling on water.

IDENTITIES

I annul time
Standing across the night
In a cluster of enchanting love
Rolling in a girl's chat pointing to the whole sky.

My day is still
Flows with my longings in a childish plot
Curling on the sand
Moving from identity to identity.

And I sing with the wind
Circle the length and breadth
Between adorning stars
Drawn in blue pencil.

AN AIR

My time is wind
Roaming among words contradicting one another
Glistering in the bustle of day
And a primeval illusion
And dark sun floats to the water's edge
And night plays
In blue language exiled from bank to bank
Like a note flowing on the page
Covered by music
With love extended in jest
Growing in the harvest of my dream
Poured out in summer's longing
And a color of gleaming earth
And light enfolded insistent on being a song.

TESTIMONY

I invent things
With temptation renewed each time
Between a poem of thought
And a poem of dream
And deceit of great silence
And deceit of the night.

Maybe the day too is illusory in the main
Rocked in space
Across the noise of the sea
And creased flowers
And circles of yellow time.

And the testimony is crowded in the poem
Turning with words dissipating on the page
Across parallel stars
And greatest fear.

MONOLOGUE

I found a love that is not consumed
Precise clear
Near- far
Gathered together among illusions
Joined at the hand of the poet
Creating sun
And a slight wind
And a flowing memory
As in a dizzying poem
And a monologue of day
Among scattered things
Clarified in such a night
Joining to all the words.

LONGING

My mother is still
Hovering at height of star chasing star
Absorbing all the words.

And the wind plays
Flows among the stains of the day
With intoxicated longing circling above water.

And she crosses a sea
With yearning catching a ridge
And with a voice echoing in me
Whispering night.

SEA BREEZE; CORNA SONNETS

(6)
I flow in a tremendous torrent of words
With great advantage
Living in an echoing summer
In the midst of a poem

Tuneful in a breaking voice
Like a sea bird
Flying in the flow of darkness
Against the fear of the curse.

And love leads me to the burble of water
In the language of God
Free

Revolving at the speed of time
Teasing memory
Exchanging sun for sun.

(8)
Love tempers with me
Against fire dripping
Like water
And color of a needless tear

In a high moment
And singular joy
Flowing in the clear biography
Amid the folds of the night.

And I hear words in the turning of day
Laughing in loneliness preserving great beauty
Clutching a poem

In the magic of the game
And in used memory
In a moment of most pure writing.

(12)
The light is faint
Slippery on a tensed street
Across the flow of water
And wide sea

Among verses of words
And the pleasure of dream
And cascades of a soul
Curled up in pain.

And I count stars
Stubborn in temptation
Crowded into a talk of love

And time bubbles
In the eruption of the poem
Twisting in the music of night.

SELF PORTRAIT

My simple language connects to the night
Twirls in the street
Across stone
And iron
And signs of people
And speech like wind
And disruptions of shade
And cracked words
Among materials joining within me
Like citations of day
And a marginal biography
Wilting in this metaphor
Turning to a point fused onto the page.

FOR GABRIEL PRIEL (2)

You write in the language of God
On such a night
Full of shadows
Rolling in the moment's vision
And warm memory
Across a star marking a star
On the most ancient street.

And I wander in the tune
Echoing riotous music
Breaking in my tipsy dream
And confused love
Darting from the dark
Cosmic hovering like the wind
Revolving in me
Dripping in tear after tear.

I AM THE POEM'S ARCHITECT

I am the poem's architect
Circling in the moment's passion
At the margins of such a sonnet
And in music playing within me
Exaggerating in longing
Breaking the dark
Flowing from bank to bank
Stealing fire
Painting in blue
Mixed in the chain of my pure words
In a most open dream
And in tune flooding me
In a cycle of love living in lasting memory
Spread on the scroll.

WATERCOLOR (2)

My language is addicted to the night
Amongst plastic toys
And things falling on the ground
With such laughter
Spontaneous
Sailing on water
In a pencil drawing
Hesitant on a street of gold and iron.

And then I wander among the shards
Open to all corners
Across the flakes of my vision
And a tree bending in the wind
Among stars flowing on high
Like God's flowers
Climbing on the bottom of the sky
Hanging between sunset and sunset.

WATER MOLECULES

I mix the molecules of water
In a flow of a dialogue
And the night's rain
Mumbling my tunes in pure thought
Like clear music crossing my poem
Echoing among the words
In the vortex of time
And great wind
And funny love stealing on the page
Rolling from yearning to yearning
With such logic
And sadness playing within me
Amid the straps of my silent memory.

A VARIATION ON A THEME
BY SALVADOR DALI

My speech is imprisoned in me
Among confused words
And funny things
Like an old memory
And a love bound in me
Marked in a tune invading the page
In blue time
Passing from memory to memory
Between silent words
In a parched poem
And a sad day
Across a black sea greater than the night
Legible in the dark
In the wind's page
Flowing on high.

GOD SITS ON HIGH

God sits on high
Binding my pure words
Among the bluest stars
Adding invention to invention
In the continuum of a dream rolling on the floor
Across stubborn music
Sinking in me
Like in a warehouse of things connecting to
memory
Pouring into water
With such love
Crowding in me
Resembling the sun
Mixed in a biography linking word to word
Insisting in being a poem
A useful talk curling in the night
Against a fading street
And time rising to heavens.

I AM A LAUGHING WOMAN

I am laughing woman
Hesitant
Born from the poem
In a blue drawing
Mystic
Clear
Across old time
And a flower clinging to the night
In the quiet of the street
Fitting me
With such memory
And hastiest writing
Alluding to my words
Combining in yearning
Across the day's clamor
And the murmur of fictive things
On a most twisted street
And with love rising silently
Insisting on being a poem.

A LILY

You sing at such a time
Burning a day
In an illusion grasping void
And writing completing the tune
Collecting words mixing in the wind
In a bundle of summer colors
And a point of pain
Resembling water music
In a talk rising in poem
In a chain of useful words
Like star
Fiction and flower
Like lament
Sand
And earth
Like a memory stone
In a most common poem
And with love crowding in me
Curling on the parchment
Silent across the murmur of the night.

A MEASURE OF LOVE

I exaggerate with words
Creating a poem on such a night
In round time
Memory-like
Preening itself in this festivity
Bearing a flower
And highest stars
Flowing in such words
Measuring my love
Pouring into water
Across the trains of light
At a moment turning in the tune
In obsessive rain
And blue sketch
Becoming in a dream
Against a net of things intersecting in me
Like a great memory
Like quick laughter
Inventing my words
In a most broken illusion.

I AM AN ARCHEOLOGIST

I am the archeologist of words
Stealing in this monologue
With the force of night
Across time turning within me
Between verses next to the dark
In a lofty liturgy
Rising at the edge of day
Fluid like a sea
Clinging to the wind
In a praise of stars
Born against the floods of water
In such a playful poem
And melancholic writing
Joining the sketch
Bursting the sun
Furling my childhood
In a most useful drawing.

AN ARCHETYPICAL POEM

My poem is archetypical
Echoing from border to border
In language touching me
With such loneliness
Across the noise of the sea
And the murmur of wind
Confused in the cycle of time
Mumbling in such speech
In confession bursting on a tablet
With tremor and weakness
And bluest dream
Curling in an illusion flowing amidst all the
revelations
In darkness wrapping itself in me
Filling the earth
Streaming in the great plain
Climbing to heaven with such yearning
Binding my pain.

A FUNNY LOVE

I live in the grayness of the night
Against a wind skimming the waters
Rolling with such a tune
In an prankish poem whispering my words
At a time of summer
Mixed among the ripples of my day
With things of desire
And a funny love cutting through me
Turning in a quick sketch
Like in exquisite drawing muttering my poem
Curling at a time drawn in me
Scorched like the sun
Woven into a dizzy thought
And a day's pain
Hard like stone.

AN OLD STREET

I create my poem
Invent words
Cut from the sun
With great revelation
Invading me
Keeping my longings amid the tricks of the wind
Against all illusions
Circling on such a night
And in music echoing on an old street
Crossing my poem
Returning to me as if from childhood
Drawing a flower
Among most used things
In tension and thunder
And lightening resembling God
Curling in such writing.

AN EXPERIMENTAL POEM

I am silent in summer
Opposite a visionary sun
And pure living--love moves on the page
Recalling memories like Proust.

And my speech is fiction playing with me
In a drawing tied to the poem
Flowing among the words
Like a tear mixing with water.

And the moment is grace
Bursting among symbols of night
Sliding wide eyed
Touching the sun.

It is hard for me to draw longing in the sand.

DIRGE

I awaken at first rain
Almost mythic
Curl up in a childish plot
Tucked away in the landscape's pall.

And then I burn night
Nihilistic bursting time
Give myself up to the wind
Diluted in a moment of grace.

And my day is periodic
A kind of metaphor tattooed into all that exists
Like mute basalt
And a dirge of the sea
And a poem of God.

ABSURDITY

My day is still
Revolving in the current
Twisting in the circle of water
Moving in the beauty of change
With a kind of absurd joy
Rising in the mouth of the poet.

And I whisper words among the shreds of wind
Curling in the wave of light
Hewn across the nothingness of night
Knowing a poem
Diluted among all fancies.

NIGHT SCROLLS

I circle among stars
In the dark burden
And distant rain
And hard rock
Revolving among the scrolls of night
Opposite eyes vanishing on high
*   nursing my poem.*

And my words wander
Flowing down a marginal street
Wasting in the matter of day
Breaking in water
In time dismantling all the illusions.

What could be absurd earns authenticity.

ABOUT THE POET

Edith Covensky was born in Bucharest, Romania, grew up in Haifa, Israel, and lives in the U.S. in Bloomfield Hills, Michigan. She has authored, to date, 30 books of poetry in mostly bi-lingual editions, Hebrew/English published by Eked and Gvanim in Israel. Among her titles are *Night Poems* (1992); *An Anatomy of Love* (1992); *Partial Autobiography* (1993); *Jerusalem Poems* (1996); *After Auschwitz* (1998); *Also Job was a Paradox* (2010); *Matters of Sand* (2012); *And On the Border of Water* (2012.) Her poetry has also been translated into Arabic, French and Romanian.

Covensky teaches since 1987 Hebrew language, literature and Israeli culture including Israeli film at the Classical and Modern Languages, Literatures and Cultures Department at Wayne State University in Detroit, Michigan. She is also editor in America of the Israeli journal *Pseifas*, dedicated to Hebrew poetry in English speaking countries.

A recording of her selected poetry read by the poet in Hebrew and English appeared in 2014 and is available through the publisher as well. This same year her Hebrew volume entitled: *Microcosmus* (Microcosm) *–Selected Poems 1992-2012* was published by Gvanim in Israel.

Edith Covensky is married to Harvey Covensky, Attorney, and has two children, Jeffrey and Laurice.

ACKNOWLEDGMENTS

Heartfelt gratitude to Kira Henschel of MavenMark Books (HenschelHAUS) for the wonderful production of the book.

Equally extended gratitude to the artists who contributed their appealing works to this book:

    Arie Menes (www.ariemenes.com)
    Michael Kovner
    Audrey Mantooth
    Alonzo Pantoja
    Peter Klett

Much appreciation as well to the two translators: Marganit Weingerger-Rotman and Edouard Codish.

ABOUT THE AUTHOR

D r. Yair Mazor is a professor of modern Hebrew literature and Biblical literature with the University of Wisconsin— Milwaukee. To date, Professor Mazor authored 28 scholarly books and over 250 articles and critical essays that have been published in USA , Israel, and numerous European countries. Dr. Mazor is well known as an invited guest lecturer and has spoken to audiences in Barcelona, Toledo, and Granada, Spain; Copenhagen and Aarhus, Denmark; Bergen, Norway; Paris, France; Prague, Czech Republic; Oxford, Cambridge, London, England; Venice, Italy; and many other venues around the world.

Among the many scholarly awards Dr.Mazor has received are the Sadan Prize and the Shpan Prize for two of his books, the Baron Prize for Excellency in the Field of Jewish Studies, the most distinguished teaching award by University of Wisconsin— Milwaukee and the Friedman Prize, a national award for the most distinguished Hebrew literature scholar in the United States.

During his military service in Israel, Dr. Mazor served as a combat paratrooper and parachuting instructor.

CPSIA information can be obtained
at www.ICGtesting.com
Printed in the USA
FFOW03n1414200715
15183FF